AWAKENING THE *World*

A GLOBAL DIMENSION TO SPIRITUAL PRACTICE

AWAKENING
THE *World*

A GLOBAL DIMENSION
TO SPIRITUAL PRACTICE

LLEWELLYN VAUGHAN-LEE

First published in the United States in 2006 by
The Golden Sufi Center
P.O. Box 428, Inverness, California 94937.
www.goldensufi.org

Printed and bound by Thomson-Shore, Inc.

Cover design by Anat Vaughan-Lee. Circular cover image "All Creation
Praises the Lord"; Nine Choirs of Angels, from the *Liber Scivias* (*Know
the Ways of the Lord*) by German mystic St. Hildegaard of Bingen
(1098-1179). Photo credit: Erich Lessing/Art Resource, NY.

Library of Congress Cataloging-in-Publication Data

Vaughan-Lee, Llewellyn.
   Awakening the world : a global dimension to spiritual practice /
   Llewellyn Vaughan-Lee.
     p. cm.
   Includes bibliographical references and index.
   ISBN 1-890350-12-5 (alk. paper)
    1. Spiritual life. I. Title.
   BL624.V378 2006
   297.4'4--dc22

                      2006043620

CONTENTS

PREFACE

Throughout this book, in an effort to maintain continuity and simplicity of text, God, the Great Beloved, is referred to as He. Of course, the Absolute Truth is neither masculine nor feminine. As much as It has a divine masculine side, so It has an awe-inspiring feminine aspect.

From what is small and fragile
let abundance and power come:
let humanity take on
the consciousness
of the whole of creation
and be absorbed
by
this task.[1]

INTRODUCTION

When one is changing,
How does one know
a change is taking place?
When one is not changing,
How does one know that a change
hasn't already occurred?
Maybe you and I are still
in a dream and
have not yet awakened.

Chuang Tsu

Fundamental changes are taking place in the inner and outer worlds. We are a part of these changes, and yet these changes also depend upon us. Our spiritual practice, our aspiration and awareness, are part of the lifeblood of the planet. There is an urgency now, a primal need, that we *live* the depths of our longing, our desire for Truth. Life is calling to us to realize our true nature and life's wholeness. We are needed to help life to awaken from a dream that is destroying it.

But if we are to live the real potential of our spiritual practice, we need to break free from the focus on our own individual journey. We need to reclaim the simple truth that spiritual life is "not about us," and open to a larger, all-embracing vision. If spiritual life is not about the whole, it has lost its true nature; it has instead been subverted by the ego and its patterns of self-concern. Everything that has been created is in service to life, to the real purpose of creation. We are not separate from life, and we need to recognize how our individual spiritual journey is part of life's sacred purpose, and how it can nourish life in different ways.

Just as the individual can forget her true nature and real purpose, as many of us have painfully experienced, so can life itself forget. Life is an interdependent living organism that reflects the collective consciousness of humanity. As humanity has become obsessed with materialism and forgotten the sacred nature of life, so has life forgotten its own sacred nature, its primal purpose of divine revelation. We need to redeem this desecration, give back to the world an awareness of its divine nature. This is the work of the mystic. The mystic, the spiritual seeker, belongs to the core of life, to the mystery of life's revelation. We carry within our spiritual centers the secrets of life, and we know the deep joy in recognizing life's need for what is real, what has been hidden within the heart. Part of our purpose is to give these secrets back to life: to help life become aware of its true nature.

Our individual inner journey is part of the world's journey. To deny this is to live inside the veil of separation. A simple awareness of oneness unites us with all of life, with every stone, every insect, every soda can crumpled in the garbage. We are life itself, breathing, suffering, rejoicing. We are the pain of the sick and the laughter of the child. We are neither better nor worse than any particle of creation. Our hunger for the source, our search for the divine, is life's hunger, life's search. We need to give our journey back to life and acknowledge the oneness that unites everything. Nothing is separate. All is He.

To take this step is to renounce many of our spiritual expectations. How often have we hoped that our journey would free us from life's difficulties, hoped to be something special, to be other than the ordinary, to become "enlightened?" The ego tries to claim everything for itself, even subverting the soul's longing for Truth into another illusion. Do we have the courage to give up these illusions, our spiritual dreams, to step into the arena of real spiritual service? Can we leave behind this seductive but limited imagined spirituality and embrace the real unknown? Do we dare to know what life and love really want from us, the vulnerability and complete participation that are needed? Here there is no bargaining, no safe place, but a giving of oneself without expectations: a response to a need that is present in every breath. Life needs our spiritual commitment; otherwise it will die, destroyed by greed and materialism, by a culture that thinks only of itself.

Every breath is a remembrance of God and an opportunity to be fully present in life. He is one and we are a part of this oneness. We are present in His world for His sake. And life is calling to us to remember our commitment, our pledge to honor what is real. Our remembrance of God is what is most precious in the world. The breath that remembers Him is His breath of life. Life needs this as a drowning man needs air.

And yet centuries of spiritual history tell us to turn away from life, to seek only the inner journey and renounce the outer. We are told of the darkness and dangers of our instinctual nature, of how we can become so easily seduced and corrupted by the world. These are stories of our forefathers who have given themselves to the eternal search for Truth. Their wisdom is real, and yet it belongs to a time that has passed. We cannot escape from the demands of the present. We cannot be deaf to life's pressing need. To be awake is to respond to the need of the moment, and in this moment the world needs us. Can we deny the call of the soul of the world?

When we respond to life's call for our spiritual commitment, we will discover that the ancient spiritual truths are also alive and changing, revealing a new face. The journey Home is not a text written in an old book, but is part of the divine mystery of life. Our longing for God and the journey Home are at the core of creation. They are part of the heartblood of life. Without the stream of souls turning towards God, life would lose its music and sacred meaning. But as the oneness of life changes and evolves, so does the way the journey presents itself. It is always the same journey, the eternal cry of the soul for its source, the lament of the reed torn from the reed-bed. But now the journey needs to acknowledge life's oneness and the interdependence of all of creation. Oneness needs to be stamped into the cells of the wayfarer, so that from the very beginning of the journey, from the moment the soul turns towards God, we honor the whole. We need to bring our turning towards God into the cells of our body, into the breath that connects us with all of life. We can no longer afford to separate the inner from the outer, the one from the many.

The path is changing. Doors in the inner worlds that used to open us to mystical secrets are being closed, while other doorways, often in the midst of life, are being opened. The path is also revealing deeper truths that until now have been kept hidden. There are spiritual teachings, ancient traditions, that have always connected the inner journey to the whole of life, that have kept the balance between the inner and outer worlds and used spiritual practices as a way of nourishing the whole. Some of these practices will gradually be revealed, their esoteric dimension adapted to the present time. Part of the purpose of this book is to point to this dimension of spiritual practice—to show, for example, how the axis of love functions at the center of the world, and how the heart connects together different levels of reality.

For centuries these have been closely guarded secrets, passed from initiate to initiate. But it is time for humanity to take more responsibility for its spiritual heritage; work that used to be done by only a select few can now be practiced by many. Times of transition are always dangerous, and maybe these truths will be misused. But humanity needs to be given the knowledge that is needed to transform the world.

This book takes the reader into the arena of spiritual service that belongs to the future. It is not a detailed map or exact description of spiritual practices. This is a time of transition in which the new ways are not yet fully formed. Instead this book outlines some of the foundations, the patterns that are developing in the inner and outer worlds, and the part we have to play in their development. It points to some of the spiritual attitudes we have to leave behind and to others that we should cultivate. It also describes some of the dangers and difficulties of this time of transition, the fault lines of our culture and the vast forces colliding beneath them. Its intent is to expand our perception of what is spiritual life, and to align the reader with the work that needs to be done.

At this time little is definite or sure. But something is alive that is changing both us and our planet, and our participation is essential. We are being asked to be present in a new way, to give ourselves in service more completely. These chapters are footsteps to a future that is already present—if we dare to open our eyes. Our Beloved is revealing Himself in a new way, and we are here to witness it, to say, "Yes. Yes. Yes!"

THE FIRST STEP

I saw my Lord in my dreams and I asked,
"How am I to find You?"
He replied, "Leave yourself and come!"

Bâyezîd Bistâmî

Take one step away from yourself and—
Behold—the path.

Abû Sa'îd ibn Abî-l-Khayr

BEYOND SELF-FULFILLMENT

The first step on the spiritual path is in many ways the
most radical and the most difficult. It is to recognize that
it is not about "me"—the journey Home, the journey
back to God, is the journey of the soul and not the ego,
not the "I." We are not the pilgrim on the path but an
obstacle to the real journey in which the soul or Self,
the substance within the heart of hearts, returns to the
Source which it never left.

How can we understand this when all we know is
the ego? We see our life through the eyes of the ego: our
life is about us. At the beginning we can only see the
spiritual journey in the framework of the ego and its
values, and so we easily imagine this journey as a process
of spiritual self-improvement leading to a deeper and
more fulfilling life. Added to this is our Western obsession
with the individual self. The values of our culture are

about individual fulfillment, whether on a material, sexual, or emotional level. We easily project these values onto the spiritual journey, and merely create a more elevated image of fulfillment. We not only want to be emotionally or sexually fulfilled; we also want "spiritual fulfillment," which we imagine to be a more deeply meaningful life. Into this dream of spiritual fulfillment we may project our images of having a guided life or a spiritually meaningful relationship, of being accepted or loved; maybe we even project the myth of "enlightenment." We cannot see beyond the horizon of ourself.

This initial image of the journey is understandable: how can we imagine something beyond ourself when the world of the ego is all that we know, when the eyes of the ego are our only means of seeing? But sadly, this image of the journey is also reflected to us by much contemporary "spiritual" literature and teaching, which promise such fulfillment. We are told that we can enjoy the fullness of life through living in the present moment; we are instructed how to love ourselves, even how to have enlightened sex. And so the spiritual world is contracted into the values of the ego and remains centered on ourself.

But is this all that we can understand? Are we so conditioned by a culture that focuses on self-gratification that we can only be attracted by further images of self-fulfillment? No longer focusing on a better material life, we may aspire towards spiritual goals, not realizing that we have just recreated a different form of self-interest, and still remain imprisoned by the ego and its endless cycle of unmet needs. Do we have to remain with these familiar patterns to comfort us? Or are we prepared to acknowledge that this greatest adventure may not be about us?

Our culture both subtly and overtly denies us the teachings and tools that can free us from its self-obsessive grip. We give so much of our lives to its demands of material prosperity that consume our time and energy. Do we also have to surrender our souls to the image of spiritual prosperity? What about the ancient truth that we can go beyond the ego with its seductions and desires, that we can escape from this *maya*? Do we dare to glimpse the vast nature of a journey that can take us far beyond our small self-centered world?

ACCESSING THE POWER OF THE DIVINE

At the present time there is another vital dimension to this question. We are aware that this is a moment of global crisis, that our current collective values, the corporate forces of materialism and greed, are destroying our planet. We may sense that spiritual awareness has an important part to play in healing and transforming our world, and that we have a real responsibility to create change before these forces irrevocably destroy both the outer and inner worlds. But how can we access our spiritual power and potential to create change when we approach spirituality with the same self-centered values that have created our global predicament?

The very nature of the ego is to see itself as separate: the development of the ego is what creates our sense of a separate self as the child becomes separate from the mother. But the ego also separates us from the divine and its all-pervading oneness. It is our basic identification with the ego that denies us access to our innate spiritual wisdom and power. This is why real spiritual paths teach us to renounce or surrender the ego and why so many present spiritual teachings are subtly corruptive—by promising us the illusion of individual fulfillment, they keep us trapped within the ego and thus deny us access to what is real. If we stay within the values of the ego, we only have access to the energy and vision of the ego, its patterns of illusion. The world cannot be healed by a spiritual illusion. But it can be healed by the real power of the divine that is within each of us.

Only the divine can heal and transform the world— the forces of antagonism in the world are too powerfully constellated for us to resolve on our own; the patterns of greed that are draining the lifeblood of the planet and destroying its ecosystem are too firmly entrenched. But we cannot have access to the energy of the divine unless we step beyond our ego-self.

The power of the divine can be understood in many different ways. It is the light of the Self, the sacred forces in creation, the real joy of life, the energy of our eternal nature, our love for God and His love for us. True spiritual traditions that look beyond the ego connect us with this power and then teach us how to bring it into life: how to live from the divine center of ourself in the midst of everyday life. They teach us how to be of service to the divine and not to the desires of the ego. These spiritual traditions also teach us that sacrifice is part of the journey. We have to "die before we die": surrender the values of the ego in order to embrace the larger dimension of the Self. Without this attitude of surrender or sacrifice there can be no real journey, nor can we live a life of true service.

With the correct attitude of spiritual service we can go beyond the ego and its limitations, and step into the dimension of our divine nature, the Self. In order to bring this quality into life, the divine needs our participation: we are the guardians of the planet. We need to work with its energy for the well-being of the whole.

Our ego-oriented life has created a fragmented world of conflict, with different factions striving for dominance. We have to compete and struggle, caught in the images of winners and losers and all of the other dramas of dualism. In this world, we have to look out for ourself because no one else will. In our separateness we also often feel alone and isolated, impotent to effect real change. Moreover, it is partly due to our self-created illusion of our separateness from the earth that we are destroying our own ecosystem. If we realized how intrinsically we are connected to the earth, we would never treat it so badly.

Once we step outside of the illusion of our own separate self, a radically different picture emerges. Our divine nature exists in a dimension of oneness. Unlike the ego, which always looks out for its own self-interest, the Self reflects a vision of oneness, in which each individual part is nourished according to its real need. A glimpse of the Self gives us a sense of an interconnected oneness in which nothing is separate: everything is an expression of a oneness that is dynamically alive. Every person, every stone is this oneness; everything is connected and interdependent. Our individual Self is the Universal Self and it is all a living organism of light and love.

When we live with a conscious awareness of our intrinsic oneness, we bring this oneness into our collective consciousness, which is dying through the illusion of separation. Our light *is* the light of the world; our divine consciousness *is* the spiritual consciousness of the world—nothing is separate. And the energy and awareness of the divine *are* within each of us, *are* each of us. When we turn away from the ego and its desires, we know that we embody this sacred substance. And we are also life, hungry for what is sacred. In the dynamic interconnected whole, we are the in-breath and out-breath of life—a life that is not just physical existence, but a multidimensional living organism of light and love. We are the spiritual lifeblood of the planet and we need to honor this dimension of life, this quality of oneness that is present within everything.

GLOBAL ONENESS AND SELF-INTEREST

We need the power of the divine with its vision of oneness in order to step from our isolated consciousness into an understanding of global wholeness. Through the eyes of the Self we discover that we are part of an interdependent physical and spiritual ecosystem in which each part nourishes and supports the whole. Our survival and evolution will depend upon our understanding the interrelationships between the parts and how they dynamically work together. The Self contains the seeds of this understanding because it always sees everything as a reflection of the whole. Our divine nature *is* the oneness of the world, which is also the oneness of God. Through a creative relationship with our higher nature we can bring an understanding of oneness into our lives, learn to live according to its principles and knowledge.

Oneness is not an abstract idea but a living expression of the divine. The oneness of all of life is a reflection of His oneness, a manifestation of the oneness that is within our own heart and soul. And just as humanity has been given and also developed a body of knowledge of how to work with our inner divine nature—how to transform ourself and realize our higher consciousness, we are also being given access now to a knowledge of how oneness works in the world. It is essential that we discover our access to this higher knowledge of life, so that life itself can be transformed. We have denied the divine nature of all of creation for too long. We have separated matter and spirit and through the power of this collective attitude have starved the world. We need to return the potency of the spirit to the world and understand how this living being really functions. We need to regain an understanding of the spiritual principles that underlie creation and how to work with these principles.

This knowledge of oneness is waiting to be accessed. It is present within the spiritual body of the earth, just as our own higher wisdom is present in our higher consciousness. But this knowledge cannot be accessed by a consciousness that is focused on the ego. It will only reveal itself to a consciousness that looks to the well-being of the whole. Sadly, because so much contemporary spiritual teaching focuses solely on our individual spiritual well-being, many people are denied access to this knowledge. They do not even know that it exists. That is why it is essential that we take the first step and recognize how we limit and isolate ourselves. In the words of al-Hallâj, "The first step is to cease isolating ourself from God."

Divine wholeness is waiting to be lived. It includes every cell of creation, the wisdom within every plant and animal. It is a deep instinctual knowing about how the world works as a living, breathing spiritual being. And it is very practical. This is not an idealistic spiritual theory but a knowing that belongs to the basic principles of life: everything is sacred and is an expression of the Creator. There is a balance and harmony within all of creation that can be discovered and lived. In this balance the real needs of life are met, even though many of our self-induced desires will have to be sacrificed. The world is not here to give us what we want: the world is an expression of divine oneness that needs us to help it to realize its full potential.

We need to regain the wisdom of previous cultures that understood that we are here to work with the divine within life. We have been given the responsibility to help creation to evolve, to be co-creators in the deepest sense. Recognizing this spiritual and ecological responsibility belongs to the next step in our collective evolution. It is partly in order to learn this that we have constellated such a precipitous global situation. Only when we take real responsibility for our planet can we avert our present ecological disaster.

This is a major shift that humanity has to make, and the global dimension of our present problems, whether ecological or terrorist, points to the need to shift into a global awareness. And yet the forces that resist any real change have drawn us into fear and isolationism. This is the real battle that is being fought. We vitally need the knowledge of oneness, but the patterns that deny us this knowledge are being reinforced. Global communication, the internet, and satellite television connect us to the whole world. But collectively we seem unable to step beyond our self-interest and embrace the oneness of life and the world. Of course there is a price for this step. In the West we will have to lose many of the privileges we have taken for ourselves. We might have to sacrifice our dominance and the greed we disguise as consumerism.

THE SPIRITUAL PRINCIPLES WITHIN LIFE

The higher principles within life are waiting to be discovered and used. As a living spiritual being, the world can function in ways that are hidden to us at present. When we see the world through the prism of our self-centered material consciousness, we are unaware of its real nature and potential. The work of those who have been given the gift and responsibility of a spiritual awareness is to become attuned to the higher potential of life. Spiritual seekers have always been pioneers, going beyond the surface values of the collective to explore a deeper reality. We have sensed or experienced dimensions within ourself that are beyond the physical, and our dreams and visions have told us how these dimensions can transform our life. Now we need to bring this awareness into the arena of global oneness, to step aside from focusing on our individual development and recognize this larger stage. Just as there is hidden knowledge and spiritual potential within each of us, there are similar qualities within the spiritual body of the earth, and it is for us to discover them—to be receptive to their unveiling.

The world is not going to be saved by politicians or corporations, but by those in service to the divine that is within themselves and within the world. Higher knowledge has always come from within, but it needs those committed to this revelation to bring it into life, to unite the inner and outer and awaken the world to its spiritual nature. Our eyes can see the plight of our world, the problems we have created. Our hearts and higher consciousness can be attuned to divine oneness and the harmony and peace that are within. Bringing together these different levels of awareness enables the inner to influence the outer.

During the past era our focus has been on a transcendent, often disembodied spirituality. As a result we have forgotten the very practical nature of our true self. In the dimension of oneness everything is included. There is nothing higher or lower, nothing that is not sacred. Spiritual knowledge belongs to the whole of life, to each cell of creation. The soul is present within the whole body of each of us and also within the body of the earth. Spiritual principles offer us a very practical way to work with the energies of life.

Our culture, based upon science and technology, may appear to present us with a tangible, definable world divorced from the vagaries of the spirit. But we have forgotten that the father of our Western culture— Parmenides, the man who invented logic, the basis of our reasoning—was a mystic who received his teaching from the Goddess.[1] Spirituality is a science of how things really are. It helps us to understand the essence of things. A spiritual understanding attunes us not only to the real meaning of our life, but also to how life comes into exis-tence and to the forces behind creation. A transcendent divinity may require abstract metaphysics, but once we return the divine to its rightful place within creation, spirituality becomes something very different: a practical way to work with the divine energy that is within creation, a way to use this energy to benefit all of life.

But before we can be given this spiritual knowledge we have to develop the correct receptive attitude. We need to expand our spiritual consciousness from the microcosm of our own inner journey into the macrocosm of life's unfolding. We can achieve this realization at the end of the inner journey, when we discover that our individual Self is the Universal Self. Or we can make this shift through a simple expansion of consciousness that acknowledges the global dimension to oneness: We are a part of the whole of life. Nothing is separate. What is within us is within the world. Within our spiri-tual consciousness are the secrets not only of our own awakening but of the awakening of the planet.

When we have an attitude of consciousness that is receptive to this dimension of spirituality, we can be given the knowledge that belongs to life's unfolding. This knowledge is waiting to be given to humanity. The world needs our help in order to evolve. This new knowledge will cover the spectrum of our lives, from new ways of healing to the use of the non-polluting energy of light as a basic power source. We will learn how the principles of oneness can take goods and materials where they are really needed around the world, and adapt our financial institutions to this new organic model. We have seen with the rapid development of the internet how such new technologies are efficient and cost-effective in ways that we could not have imagined.

Esoteric knowledge that belongs to the spiritual awakening of our planet will also be given to us. Without this inner core of spiritual teachings all the other developments will only function on the surface and at a fraction of their real potential. The awakening of the spiritual body of the earth will enable us to understand life in a completely new way, founded upon oneness rather than division. It will give us access to power sources within the world that are needed for our development. And as the world comes alive, humanity and the planet will interrelate in a completely new way.

The spiritual body of the earth is a macrocosm of the spiritual body of the individual and follows similar ways of awakening. It cannot be forced but requires an understanding of the energies within the world and within the individual and of how they interrelate and resonate with each other. This belongs to a new level of spiritual awareness that will be given to humanity. Each era of the world and humanity's evolution requires a new body of spiritual knowledge, and as Christ said at the beginning of the last era:

And no man putteth new wine into old bottles: else the new wine doth burst the bottles, and the wine is spilled, and the bottles will be marred: but new wine must be put into new bottles.[2]

This means that each era requires a new attitude to contain the spiritual teachings that are being given. That is why the first step is to leave behind our present spiritual conditioning that focuses on our own journey. Only then can we be receptive to this new dimension of spiritual knowledge.

SPIRITUAL MATURITY

When it is time for stillness, stillness;
in the time of companionship, companionship;
at the place of effort, effort.
Everything at its time and its place.

Naqshbandi Saying

Around us is an unending revelation. In every instant
the divine is being born anew. And yet at this moment
in our history we are also at the beginning of a new era;
a new pattern of life is coming into being. Our spiritual
awareness is central to this birth. In our hearts, in our
consciousness, and with every breath, we are midwives to
a new awakening of the earth that is taking place now. In
order to participate fully in this birth, we have to leave
behind old patterns, old ways of walking on the earth
and of looking towards heaven. We are stepping into an
era of oneness that will bring together matter and spirit,
feminine and masculine, and our spiritual practice must
reflect this new alignment. We cannot renounce the
earth or follow a patriarchal model of spiritual progress.
Our soul's journey is part of the journey of the whole
of creation. Our heart is connected to the heart of the
world. Our remembrance is the remembrance of the
world. Through our awakening the world can awaken.

And yet the individual journey of the soul back to the Source, the lover back to the Beloved, continues as it always has. Everything changes and nothing changes. The journey of a soul going Home is like the spiritual heartbeat of the world. When a seeker turns towards the Beloved, all of creation rejoices, because this is the final journey for all of life. Every atom longs to be united with its Beloved, and as spiritual wayfarers we live this longing with our whole being. This journey is our greatest contribution to life and to the Beloved. We offer ourselves on the altar of His love and live His drama of separation and union.

As we expand our spiritual consciousness to include the whole of creation, it is important to remember the simplicity and ordinariness of the soul's journey. The heart's longing for God belongs to the primal essence of life. Just as a sunflower follows the sun, so does our soul look to its Source. To live and breathe this true calling often means having to leave behind many of the illusions that we may have about spiritual life.

THE INNOCENCE OF AWAKENING

At the beginning of the journey a spark of pure love touches our heart and we awake for an instant to the wonder of our real nature and our innermost relationship with the divine. Without this gift of love there would be no journey, no desire to return to God. We would remain within the clouds of forgetfulness, never knowing our true self. This spark brings us alive and turns our attention towards the journey of the soul, the greatest adventure.

Traditionally called "the turning of the heart," this awakening of love is like a first romance, except that this is no idealized lover, no romantic fantasy; this is the great love affair of the soul with God, bursting into consciousness. And yet it often evokes in the lover a similar quality of adolescent impetuousness, creating spiritual fantasies that, like their romantic counterparts, often spin out of control. It is not always easy to reconcile this awakening to real love with the mundanities of our everyday life, or to contain this innermost desire within our ordinary consciousness.

The turning of the heart awakens a fire within us. Ultimately this is the fire that will burn and consume us, transform our lead into gold. But at the beginning it is just a crazy passion that has no container. We may identify it as "longing for God," but we have no notion of the real dynamics of the journey, the painful work upon the shadow and the slow grinding down of the ego that belong to the initial years of the quest. Just as the romantic experience of falling in love does not prepare us for the real work of a relationship, the spark that touches us in the heart of hearts does not make us think of the vast and dangerous nature of what is happening. We are thrown into the love affair with God as a blind person into an infinite ocean.

This is the way it has always been. We come with innocence and longing, confused by doubts and insecurities, filled with a desire for something we cannot understand. Nor do we know what to do with the intensity and passion of the soul. What can we do except create spiritual fantasies, images of some spiritual world filled with what is unfulfilled within us?

Maybe the journey will give us the partner we have always wanted, the work we feel we deserve. We so easily project our personal needs onto the unknown potential of the quest, looking for a parent to love us, a lover to embrace us, friends to understand us, work to fulfill us.

In the West this natural tendency towards projection is augmented by a conditioning that promotes instant gratification and tells us we have the right to personal happiness. The long hard road of real spiritual training has little place in our collective consciousness.

The difficulty is compounded by the fact that at the beginning we are shown something that is immediate, belonging to the eternal Now. We are given a glimpse of what is here always, our eternal Beloved. There is no time in this moment, no long and arduous journey. Instead there is something spontaneously and completely alive. He seduces us by giving us a taste of what is already within us—the gift of ourselves as we eternally are. How can the ego with its restrictions in time and space understand or live this eternal Now?

The wayfarer does not initially understand that the real work on the path is not to have access to spiritual or mystical experiences; these are given through grace. The work is to create a container for them, so they can come alive in our daily life. An aspect of this container is the ability to discriminate between a real inner experience and a spiritual illusion created by the ego. Without a container of discrimination the wayfarer easily becomes lost and wastes the energy and potential of her awakening.

SPIRITUAL ILLUSIONS

This does not mean one should dismiss the excitement and fire of one's awakening. Traditionally this is one's spiritual rebirth, the moment the real life of the soul begins. The "yes" that until now has been hidden within the soul comes to the surface, sometimes exploding into our outer world. There are a joy and an intensity that belong to this moment, that need to be lived. Real love has arrived; real light is present. Something tremendous has begun. There can be a sense of "coming home," for the first time in one's life, of being where one truly belongs. Every phase of the path has its place; "there is a time for everything under the sun."

I remember the intensity of my own awakening, the world suddenly sparkling with a hidden light, the joy and wonder of it all. I remember my first experiences in meditation, my first experiences of an inner reality beyond the mind. I was given something I had always longed for but did not know existed. I was given a taste of what is real in the midst of a world of illusions and lies. The desire for Truth was ignited and I knew what I wanted. I had no container for the crazy passion that possessed me: it drove me almost to madness; I fasted beyond what my body could bear. But for the first time I was completely alive.

Hopefully one finds a teacher or a path to begin the work of creating a container, of channeling the fire in the right direction, so that one can live a balanced life. It was three years before I found the path that would take me Home, and I arrived there in a state far from balanced, hanging on through will and determination, thin, hungry, and with my feet hardly touching the ground. But we are each given the experiences we need, and I do not regret the craziness of those initial years, even though I know now that much of my energy and most of my actions were misplaced. For example, I had to realize that one cannot fast the body into perfection, or reach reality by force of will.

One of the dangers of the early years is spiritual illusions. We are gripped by a longing, a primal hunger for something we cannot name and do not know. We are awakened for an instant to a reality that has little echo in our outer life or inner thought-patterns. We have no context for what is actually taking place, and so naturally we create images and expectations of the path. The moment I saw the light in my teacher's eyes, I wanted to be in that space beyond the limitations of a world that I found increasingly alienating and problem-filled. I imagined that spiritual life was to live in that formless dimension of presence and love. I little imagined how the path would force me back into this world of limitations.

Many seekers fall into this illusion of escape from ordinary reality at the beginning of the journey. As one friend describes it, "I thought that I would be taken out of life. That ordinary, outer life would fade away somehow, that I wouldn't have to be responsible in life. I thought I would be lost in love. That I wouldn't have to exist as a 'separate' individual any more, that I would always be swept away in love. I thought I would be taken deeper and deeper into states of love and bliss. That it would be like going farther and farther into meditation. I really didn't think I would ever have to come back into normal life, or normal awareness."

Another friend thought that her problems would no longer exist, that they would fade away or she would rise above them to exist in a higher reality. Other seekers create the illusion that they will acquire special spiritual knowledge, or even spiritual powers. The promise of "enlightenment" is a common delusion, one that overlooks the basic truth that the ego does not have any higher experiences and that in the dimension of the Self there is no "I" to realize anything. So many illusions, so many ways we use images of the path as a way to escape from life and from ourselves. The real path takes us back to ourselves and into life. If we do not come back into ourselves, the important psychological work—the confrontation with our own darkness, the shadow, and other inner dynamics that help create the container of a balanced psyche—would never be done.

As we work upon ourself, we begin to see that many of the initial illusions of the path have to do with our experience of the ego as the sole actor in our life. One friend understood that her illusions "are all born from the obvious fact that a 'person' comes to the path, so everything I initially expected referred back to the 'personal.' For example, I thought 'I' or the 'personal self' would be in love all the time. I didn't realize that love just *is*. That it has nothing really to do with 'me,' but it just exists."

At the beginning all that we know is the ego, and so we imagine the path and its experiences through the eyes of the ego, with all its desires and images of fulfillment. Even if we have read or been told that the ego "has to go," that you have to "die before you die," we cannot imagine a state in which the "I" is not at the center. When we think of the Self, we imagine a spiritualized ego. We are rarely prepared for the simplicity of what *is*. The Self may have a cosmic dimension, but it is also the most ordinary and simple essence, a quality of being that is present in everything. And the states of non-being that exist beyond the Self we cannot begin to comprehend with a consciousness that is centered on its own sense of existence. How can we imagine a state in which we are where we are not?

While some illusions center on an inner spiritual state, others reflect a desire to manifest something in the outer, for example becoming a healer or even a spiritual teacher, having a "destiny" that we think reflects our unique spiritual nature. While some wayfarers may be called down these paths, the wish for them is often just a new form of ego-gratification, in which the ego gets hold of a pure energy or intention and uses it for its own purposes. The ego loves to inflate itself, make itself the central actor on every stage. It can be disillusioning to realize that the Self often does not need any specific outer form or role to manifest, that it is a state of being rather than a "manifest destiny."

Another common form of spiritual illusion is the idea of living a "guided life" or being in a state in which actions simply arise by themselves without the need for us as the "doer." Although there are such states in which the Self or our divine nature lives through us, they require far more conscious discrimination than we realize at the beginning. Except in rare instances of highly evolved spiritual beings, our higher nature needs to manifest through our ego and lower nature, which likes to divert the higher energy for its own purposes. "The ego lurks around every corner," seeking to subvert our true nature. We must learn to distinguish between the real need of the moment and a hidden desire or a pattern of self-protection that has taken on a spiritual form. Often the illusion of being guided is an avoidance of real responsibility for our life and actions. It is a perfect excuse for someone who does not want to fully embrace everyday life with its difficulties and demands. Patriarchal spirituality may have stressed the transcendent nature of the Self, but the Self is also an intrinsic part of life, and it can only be fully incarnated and lived when we take full responsibility for life as it is. One can only realize the Self with the full acceptance of one's life and destiny. In the words of the Sufi master Abû Sa'îd ibn Abî-l-Khayr, "Whatever is to be your fate, face it!"

Finally, the path takes us to a place where the ego surrenders and the Self becomes the ruler. Then life takes on the quality of a blank sheet of paper for the Beloved to use as He wills. But by the time we have reached this stage, we have taken full responsibility for our life, for the ego and its needs and demands. We have become mature wayfarers who do not use the path to avoid life's difficulties. We have learned the value of common sense, and learned how to live in both worlds. And we have developed constant vigilance against the ego and its cunning ways of self-deception.

ORDINARY LIFE

Perhaps no illusion is more common or more insidious than the illusion that spiritual life will take the seeker away from ordinary life. Ordinary life will always be included. In fact, we become more and more immersed in the ordinary: we "chop wood and carry water."

Often it is the mundanity of the path for which we are least prepared. After a taste of the passion of the soul, which initially seems so "other" to our common experience, we tend to expect the banality of life to fade away in the excitement or ecstasy of the inner journey. We may imagine a spiritual life filled with dramatic challenges and spiritual states. But that is simply the ego yet again co-opting the experience for its own ends. Just to be an ordinary wayfarer walking a dusty path Home is not so gratifying.

The true uniqueness of our nature often appears most ordinary and simple. As one friend describes her experience, "I am always shocked by how ordinary things are, how I keep coming *down* into the ordinary. I really expected things to seem extra-ordinary." Another friend who came to be with my teacher expected to live a simple life of meditation, but within a few years she found herself teaching in an inner-city primary school, with thirty children demanding her attention all day long. It was not what she imagined!

Often the attachment to the "extra-ordinariness" of spiritual life is another way to protect ourselves from life, or from ourself, just as a romantic fantasy can protect us from the vulnerability and demands of a real relationship. True love makes us naked and vulnerable, as the patterns that protect us are dissolved or burned away. Unlike most illusions, the real nature of the path is about becoming emptier, having less rather than more. While illusions often inflate the ego with images of being special, on the real path we become more ordinary and simple.

When we feel we are living the passion of the soul, torn apart by love, we can easily dismiss the importance of paying our bills on time, of taking care of our human needs and responsibilities. We can go through life with little attention to how we treat others, and how we treat ourselves. But without a firm ground in the ordinary, without learning how to relate to life with the attention and respect it needs, we cannot fully live the energy of the soul *here*.

A focus on ordinary life grounds the energy of the path, and also makes it more difficult for the ego to create spiritual fantasies. This is why traditionally when a young man first came to a Sufi *tekke*, or *khânqâh* (Turkish and Persian for "Sufi center or hospice"), he was given the most mundane or debasing tasks, for example cleaning the latrines, sweeping the courtyard. For the first few years he might be given no spiritual practices at all, only simple tasks of service.

It is important to not reject the ordinary dimension of our experience, because the nature of the soul is ordinary and simple, and often expresses itself in what is most ordinary. The soul is a quality of being in which things just *are*. Here peace *is*, love *is*, even power just *is*. We will never notice, let alone really live, these qualities of the soul if we follow our desires to escape the ordinary, if we create unnecessary dramas or fantasies. Zen haiku often reflect this simplicity. The dew on the grass is present in the moment without any drama. The full harvest moon on the water is both simple and profound. The container we are creating on the path is a mature relationship with life. We will never be able to live the paradox of how the ordinary and extraordinary come together if we are not willing to accept life as it is.

The real work is to stay true to ourself with all the demands of everyday life, to keep the inner attention, even for five minutes a day, when there are so many distractions. Remembrance is no longer performed in seclusion, but in the office and the supermarket. The path may be the opposite of what we expect; it may be paradoxical, confusing, and contrary to our conditioning, but it needs to be lived in this world, to be part of everyday life.

And at this particular stage in the evolution of humanity, the ordinariness of life has a new meaning. In the era now dawning, it will be able to reflect the numinosity of the soul in a new way. But in order to allow life to reflect the richness and eternal nature of the soul, we must let go of patterns both personal and collective that turn us away from the ordinary. We need to learn to discriminate between a Disneyland fantasy of spiritual life, full of roller-coaster rides and cotton candy, and the real way He is revealing Himself.

LEARNING DISCRIMINATION

We cannot avoid having illusions about the path. The power of longing and of the desire for Truth uses our imagination to draw us into a deeper experience, just as the energy of physical desire creates sexual images to attract us. The imagination creates spiritual fantasies that

we later have to reconcile with the reality of our experience, just as we have to reconcile romance with a real
relationship, but these fantasies pull us beyond ourselves.
In fact, the energy of sexuality is part of the same *kundalini*
power that pulls us towards Reality; certain spiritual and
sexual fantasies have a similar quality of love and bliss,
of being enraptured and taken. We cannot escape the
potency of the imagination that takes a nameless desire
and creates images of its fulfillment. We need the desire
to draw us out of ourselves into the vaster ocean of real
love; the illusions the imagination creates out of it can
provide the lure. To quote Ibn al-Fârid:

> For in illusion's drowsy dream
>   the phantom shadow
>   leads you to what shimmers
>   through the screens.[1]

We project our desire for the unknowable through our
imagination. We create images that can entice us along
the journey. The danger arises when we mistake the images for the real goal, when we take what is relative to
be what is absolute. Then we are getting trapped by our
fantasies, rather than being led beyond them to their real
source, the innermost desire of the heart.

At the beginning we don't recognize the real qualities
of the path—what we should cultivate or aspire to and
what we should recognize as illusion. We can't discriminate between the imaginings that draw us further in the
heart's love affair and the ego's ploys to waylay us. We
are so easily caught by the subtle mirages of the ego and
the mind. The unconscious, which can collude with the
ego, also has its powerful and seductive means to stop us
from becoming more conscious, to keep us under its spell
and patterns of dependencies. This is one of the reasons

that it is necessary to have a teacher, to help us through this self-created maze. Gradually we develop our own discrimination; we learn how to distinguish between the voices of the ego and the Self. But at the beginning we are naively deceived by the many illusions the ego creates, the many false images of the path. We do not realize how easily the ego can masquerade as our spiritual nature and trick us again and again.

There are tools that we can develop to help us discriminate, to look beneath the surface of these images of the path. For example, we can ask ourselves, does this really help me to gain or lose something, or is it just going to make me feel good? Who is it really who wants this? Does it feed into my psychological patterns, my defense mechanisms, or does it take me beyond myself, make me more free, maybe more vulnerable, help me to participate more fully? Often it is useful to discriminate between a need and a desire. Is this something I need, either for my life or the path, or does it belong to the desire-creating nature of the ego?

Unfortunately there are no exact rules; we are each unique and the path will reflect this uniqueness. There is a time to struggle to achieve what we want and a time to give up any desire, a time to be strong and a time to surrender one's strength. Sometimes what seems spiritual is the greatest deception, while what might seem a worldly illusion, for example the longing for a successful career, may help us to claim what belongs to our real nature. Sometimes even the desire for a holiday or a new car is what we actually need. Maybe we are tired, need a change, or cannot continually put energy into a car that is always breaking down. Simple common sense is often our best guide.

PATIENCE

Gradually the path and the teacher strip away our illusions, leaving us with ourself, what T.S. Eliot calls

> A condition of complete simplicity
> Costing not less than everything.[2]

The ego remains, because one cannot easily live in this
world without an ego, any sense of a separate "I." And
with the ego remain our bundle of psychological problems, the difficulties of life, the conflicts of this world.
Maybe we glimpse another reality where these problems
do not exist; maybe we sense the eternal presence of a
dimension where there is no conflict, only all-embracing
peace and love. But just as in this world we remain in
the physical body with its aches and pains, so we remain
with an imperfect ego. The real work on the path is to
balance the ego with this vaster reality that is within us
and all around us.

   The path helps us to develop the qualities we need
for this work, qualities that give us the strength and
compassion to live in a world that is imperfect, where
His presence is often veiled. Patience, along with similar qualities of tolerance, endurance, and constancy, is
central among the qualities required to cross the endless
deserts of the path. The Sufi stresses the value of patience;
the acquisition of patience, *sabr,* is a station on the Sufi
path. The station of *sabr* is associated with the spiritual
maturity that we need for a long journey during which
we have to bear the burdens and difficulties of a life of
seeming separation.[3] A story told by the tenth-century
Sufi master, Sarrâj, illustrates this as the most difficult
form of patience—the patience of enduring His absence:

A man stood before Shiblî (God's compassion upon him) and said to him: "Which act of patience is hardest for one who is patient?"

Shiblî said: "Patience in God."

"No," the man said.

Shiblî said: "Patience for God."

The man said: "No."

Shiblî said: "The patience with God."

"No," he said.

Shiblî grew angry and said: "Damn you, what then?"

The man said: "Patience without God Most High."

Shiblî let out a scream that nearly tore apart his spirit.[4]

Are we prepared to wait the endless days, months, even years when He veils Himself from us? Are we prepared to carry our devotions through this desert? Are we prepared to want nothing for ourself, knowing that He will come to us when He wills? Or do we remain caught in patterns of self-gratification, knowing only our own desires, our own dynamics of control?

One friend found it very hard to accept that even if she had found a teacher and worked to develop all the correct attitudes, there was no guarantee that He would reveal Himself, that the doors of union would open. The love affair with God is very different from pleasing a parent, where the correct behavior will bring love or attention. The path is not dependent upon our own efforts; He takes us to Him in His own way, as He wills. But to accept that we are so vulnerable and dependent upon Another, that "Allâh guides to Allâh whom Allâh will," can be hard, especially for a Western consciousness that is conditioned to value individual effort above surrender.

For many years on the path we have to learn to wait, knowing only our ego and its inadequacies. This can be a very painful and testing part of the journey, for which we need patience and perseverance. Sometimes it is easier to stay focused on the path and one's practices when there are obvious challenges in the inner or outer world to face. The endless monotony of days without Him, when there is just ordinary life that has little seeming spiritual content, can be more difficult. But it is during this time that many of our early illusions fall away, as there is little in the outer or inner to sustain them.

THE REAL WORK

The real work of the path is to be able to live the energy and higher consciousness of the Self in everyday life. Initially the Self with its energy of self-realization bursts into our ordinary consciousness, sometimes creating psychological imbalance. The ego and mind respond to this influx of energy by creating illusions, often ungrounded images of spiritual life. Gradually the ego ceases to be inflated by this new energy; the path and psychological work of confronting and integrating the shadow and other inner dynamics provide a balanced psyche, a container for our higher consciousness.

The complete surrender of the ego to the Self takes many years, and not everyone achieves this state. Rather, its structure is changed so that it learns to co-exist with the Self. It no longer constantly fights or undermines our true nature, nor is it so influenced by unconscious patterns. It ceases to be an autonomous center of consciousness, but begins to live a life of service in relation to the Self. We learn to listen, discriminate, and be guided by what is real. The ego also subtly changes as it is permeated with the light of the Self, becoming more transparent, able to transmit rather than obscure our higher consciousness.

The mind also adjusts to a higher center of consciousness. The Sufi work of "hammering the mind into the heart" describes a process in which the mind learns to work with our higher consciousness within the heart. For example, the mind learns to be attentive to, rather than rejecting, its hints. No longer so dominated by rational thought-patterns, we become more receptive to intuition. True intuition does not follow sequential thought processes, but comes from the higher Self where all knowledge exists as a state of oneness. Spiritual dreamwork helps in this training, teaching attentiveness to images and messages that come from beyond the lower mind. As we learn to listen to these dreams, we move beyond the restrictions of the ego and rational thought.

Our physical body and our instinctual nature also change, as they too become permeated by the light of the awakened Self. Sometimes processes of purification are necessary, changes of diet or habits; for example, it is important not to indulge in indiscriminate sex or more than the occasional drink, or to frequent bars.[5] But too much purification—for example excessive fasting, or even too much meditation—can also be an obstacle, as it can make one too sensitive to be able to fully participate in the dense material world of the present time. Spiritual maturity is learning to live a balanced life.

Hopefully, we have the life experiences and learn the outer skills the Self needs in order to manifest in the world: we learn our worldly craft. For example, if the Self can be of most service in the field of psychology, we study and train in this discipline. Or if the Self needs us to work in business, we might need to pursue an MBA or an apprenticeship in business. The Self does not need a vehicle full of spiritual fantasies but one grounded in a practical discipline that it can use, whether this is as a banker, musician, or therapist. It is a misunderstanding that fulfilling one's spiritual destiny requires an outer form that is "spiritual." The Self is not limited by our perceptions of what is spiritual. It embraces all of life and draws us towards the correct vehicle for our higher nature.

In the midst of life our ego, indeed our whole nature, changes, becoming subtly permeated with the presence of the Self, with an energy not full of demands and desires but of another quality altogether. At the beginning we may not recognize this other, because it is so simple and ordinary. This is our true nature alive in every moment. Often it is others who first notice a change. They might see that we are more at peace with ourselves, that we are not so gripped by conflict or negative emotions. It happens so gradually that it can be a while before we even realize that something fundamental is different. So many expectations of the path have fallen away. Others we have had to surrender painfully. And then the real path comes alive within us. We have developed a sense of who we are that is founded not upon the ego, its fears and insecurities, but upon deeper, more real qualities.

At times we may miss the impetuousness of the early years, the intensity and excitement of waking up, the dreams of spiritual states. And after losing so many illusions, what have we found? It is for each of us to discover what we have been given, what is real within us, to know "who we are, from where we have come and to where we are going."

BEYOND THE EGO

Through the grace of the path and our own efforts, we create a container that enables us to live in relationship to our higher Self. The ego and Self come into balance. Although we may still have inner obstacles, resistances that need our attention, we are living the life of the soul rather than just the ego. We have accepted the limitations of life, and know that real service is in responding to the need of the moment, not in living some imagined spiritual destiny. We have given up our visions of enlightenment, to become grounded in everyday life. Maybe in meditation, or in the midst of life, we have occasional glimpses of a different reality, a sense of overwhelming peace, or a deep joy that is present. Occasionally our heart is filled with an inexplicable sweetness; we see the love that is in every leaf on every tree. But then the veils fall again, and we are back in the world of the ego.

Is this the whole journey? When Dhû-l-Nûn asked, "What is the end of love?" he was told, "O simpleton, love has no end, because the Beloved has no end." The states of love continually change. When we have finally accepted the ordinariness of the path, sometimes He laughs and bewilders us, turning our world upside down, opening us to His grandeur and majesty. Once again our image of the path is destroyed, and we are thrown beyond ourself. Once again we realize that a deeper degree of surrender and not knowing is required. One friend described how this happened to her:

> In a dream I was told that I have to prepare to die now. Quite soberly, and there was no reaction in me. It was just what it was, and when I recollected the dream, it still was like a sober thought.

Then a few days later I had an experience in which I was told: "You will be dying soon. Be prepared." Again there was no reaction, no emotion. I took it seriously. I thought, I have to arrange some things, so I don't leave too much chaos. I have to clear things, papers... soon. It felt like being sent on a journey where you just have to go, because you have to do something there.

But the next day I had this experience. I was moving at an unbelievable speed through space. Extremely fast. Who was I? "I" was not I, but an energy or a kind of consciousness I participated in. I moved towards a black sun that was radiating so intensely. It was the innermost, the absolute center, and it just pulled me. I realized that it was the intensity of this pull that made the speed, that was moving me so fast. I came closer and closer, I began to dissolve. There was just this endless sweetness of a burdenless "weakness," and then even this feeling was being absorbed, everything was absorbed. But—I don't know how it could happen—at the same moment "I" was being broken, blown up, exploded in thousands and thousands of pieces. I kind of fainted, lost consciousness, and then coming back found "myself"—this consciousness that I could feel—everywhere. Really everywhere, in each drop of the ocean, in every human face, in stones and stars.

I was shaken, also physically. In the following days I found myself trembling. Feeling very dizzy, I hardly could keep balance. I had to hold on to the counter when I was buying food; everything was turning around for days. And it is not only the physical balance. I am thrown between extreme states of feeling so totally vulnerable—and there is incredible pain—and the ecstatic feeling of joy, of coming home, of freedom....Sometimes I think now definitely I am mad, I am going crazy. But there is nothing that wants to change it. Like in the experience, I feel being pulled and pulled, and it is where I want to go.

It is impossible to think about what I experienced, to think with the mind—I tried to, in order to understand what is not to be understood, this all-breaking thing that in the depth of union, of oneness, of finally nothing, there was this bursting into pieces, the nothingness exploding into creation, it is such a shock....

Everything seems to be different. The whole of existence is something so thin, such a thin veil, similar to this physical body that I sense as so fragile...I don't know why I try to write it down—whatever I put into words it isn't the real.

This is not a spiritual fantasy, but a real experience that leaves you with nowhere to stand. Everything you know, all sense of self and stability, is destroyed in an instant. Without all the years of preparation, of learning to be grounded, without the subtle but strong container that has been created, one would go completely crazy. Then the experience could not be lived, but would just spin out of orbit, throwing you far beyond the stars, unable to return to any balanced life. This friend has a family, children who need her attention. She could not retreat to a cave to sit immersed in non-being, in the bliss of complete absorption. She has to get up in the morning, take the children to school, cook the dinner, and help them with their homework.

The path prepares you for such an experience, which comes when you least expect it. When the teacher or a superior on the path knows you are ready, that you are able to bear it, you are completely drawn out of the ego, pulled towards the real center and beyond. Is this death or life? You return dazed and unknowing. But something fundamental has changed. The dark core of non-being, the "black sun," has absorbed you. The ego as the center of consciousness has been forever annihilated, and you realize the fragility of its existence, of life as you knew it.

Is this the end or the beginning? These are just words. To be where you are not is a paradoxical statement until you have lived it, and then it makes complete sense. And still you return to "everyday life," and although the ego is changed, it also remains. Spiritual maturity is to live as a mystic in the world, being fully responsible in our everyday life even though you know the world is a fragile illusion. And in the inner worlds, other currents are flowing, powerful forces that come from beyond the stars. Sometimes these currents bring sweet fragrances, sometimes they are cold and desolate and howl through you. There are vast darknesses and oceans of light. But we have been trained to stay centered, holding onto the thin thread that is suspended between the worlds. The eleventh-century master al-Kharaqânî was asked,

> "Who is the appropriate person to speak about *fanâ* (annihilation) and *baqâ* (permanence)?" He answered, "That is knowledge for the one who is suspended by a silk thread from the heavens to the earth when a big cyclone comes and takes all trees, houses, and mountains and throws them in the ocean until it fills the ocean. If that cyclone

is unable to move him who is hanging by the silk thread, then he is the one who can speak on *fanâ* and *baqâ*."

COLLIDING FORCES

And now we stare astonished at the sea,
And a miraculous strange bird shrieks at us.

W. B. Yeats[1]

THE FAULT LINE

Collectively we are walking along a fault line. There are vast pressures building up under our feet, primal powers in the depths which have been moving for centuries. We feel tensions in the air around us, the conflicts of terrorism, the threat to the ecosystem. But within the ground, greater forces are building, forces that belong to the future and not the present. Mostly we walk unknowingly, sensing something but having little knowledge of these vaster forces that will shape our collective destiny.

The fault line on which we are walking is the place where two eras meet. When one era ends and another begins, forces of a whole different magnitude collide. Because these energies move so slowly, constellating over centuries, we do not recognize the enormous scale of what is taking place.

A physical earthquake occurs when two geological plates collide. The fault line is where the plates meet and the pressure erupts, breaking through the fragile surface of the earth that up to that moment seemed so immovable. A different earthquake will come as the forces of the inner world break through the surface structures of our lives. The inner forces of our individual and collective unconscious are as powerful and as hidden as the physical forces that create continents. Sometimes they erupt in the collective psyche in wars and migrations, shaping our collective destiny. They can cause immense suffering, as in the world wars, or bring freedom, as in the sudden fall of the Berlin Wall and the end of communism in Europe.

What will happen when such an earthquake comes? How will we respond? We know that our present patterns of response are inadequate. We have experienced our reactions to the disturbances in our world: how we contract around our fear and cling to our possessions in order to protect our "way of life." But what if the very earth that we stand on, on which we have built our lives, begins to move? Will we be able to find more adequate, more productive ways of responding?

Many talk of a new age, a new era of global consciousness. But few understand the magnitude and power of the changes taking place. Mostly we notice the surface changes—new diseases, the depletion of the ozone, increased terrorism, an unstable economy, a new war in a foreign land. But these are just symptoms of something deeper, like the changing patterns of birds in flight before a storm.

In fact there are real signs around us, but they are written in a language we mostly have forgotten. And we cannot imagine what they are telling us, because the shifts that are taking place have not happened for so long that we do not have the images in our collective memory, except in myths of when the gods walked among us.

Sometimes a poet may glimpse a truth and use his craft to translate the signs, as Yeats did when he wrote,

> Turning and turning in the widening gyre
> The falcon cannot hear the falconer;
> Things fall apart; the center cannot hold…
>
> Surely some revelation is at hand;
> Surely the Second Coming is at hand….
> And what rough Beast, its hour come round at last,
> Slouches towards Bethlehem to be born?[2]

Yeats sensed that something was falling apart and something was waiting to be born. But he had only the images of the past to translate his vision. And the past is not what is happening. What is falling apart is the very fabric of our life, but what is to be born comes from the beyond, from a new dimension of being. That is why we find it so difficult to read the signs that are all around us. We can feel the pressure that is building, the fault line in the midst of our material culture. But we have no sense of the real intensity of power that is building up beneath the surface, and no knowledge of the purpose of this power.

SIMPLE ANSWERS

When one era ends and another begins, power is generated to bring the new era into being. The power is needed to help dissolve the images and structures of the past, to destroy what is old and help the new to be born.

Collectively, we must let go of many patterns and ways of relating if we are to embrace an entirely new way of being and living together. For example, we will have to move beyond the sense of security we have tied to material prosperity. Attachments around money and material goods will have to give way to a deeper source of safety and well-being if we are to move with the changes that are coming.

Our outdated patterns are already losing their hold on us. Many sense this, and are feeling a deep anxiety around issues of security. But are we looking closely at the source of this anxiety? Do we recognize the changes that are possible? Are we allowing the old to fall apart, to reveal the new?

Despite deep fears of terrorism and economic or environmental threats, the anxiety that is present in our culture does not come from any outside force. The real problems we are facing are not political, sociological, or even ecological. Rather, we are sensing that something in our foundation no longer holds. This is the deep reason for our collective unease, which we project onto outer forces that appear to threaten us.

It is time to look closely at what is really happening. The mystic has always known that in order to find the cause of any effect we have to turn our attention inward—to look at the inner patterns. We look to the hints in our dreams; we read the images of our psyche that are not censored by our conscious conditioning. When Joseph interpreted the dreams of the seven years of plenty and the seven lean years, Egypt was saved from a catastrophe.

And yet we have rejected the images of the inner as belonging to a mythological past or the psychiatrist's couch. Instead, we listen to the voices of the outer experts. But with so many newscasters, political and economic analysts, and even spiritual teachers, how do we know whom and what to trust? And do we even know how to listen?

If we look carefully, we can find a thread that links it all together—links our dreams and the stories on the news, links the trivial, the mundane, and the sensational. There is a thread that is our collective destiny, and it is inside each of us as well as in the world around us.

This thread is so simple it is overlooked. It is so ordinary we pass it by. It is in our hope, in our need to be loved, in the warmth of a handshake or the touch of a kiss. It is in the most basic connection between human beings, not the words we say but the very nature of communication. It is in the simple fact that we all live together, whether in the slums or the suburbs. It is in the primal knowing that we are one.

NEW CONNECTIONS

Because we live at the end of an era, life has apparently become more complex. This is one of the signs of things falling apart. With our computer-generated models we look for complex answers to our problems.

The signs of the emerging culture are not complex. They are in patterns that unify, that bring things together, rather than destroy and break things into myriad pieces. The danger arises when we turn away from what is of-fered, through either ignorance or arrogance—when we stick to our models of ever-increasing complexity rather than recognize the simple human values that belong to our being.

We do not have to save or protect our culture. We do not have the power to resist the dynamics of change. Nor do we have to create a new culture. We have neither the energy nor the knowledge for such an undertaking.

But we do have a responsibility: to listen, to love and be loved, and to become aware of what is really happening. We have to accept that *we* cannot save the planet, just as we cannot defeat the forces of corruption. Enough battles have been fought, and the planet is a living being that can heal itself, with our love and cooperation.

What we always seem to overlook is the simple wonder of being human, which means to be divine. We are the meeting of the two worlds, the place where miracles can happen and the divine come alive in a new way. We are the light at the end of the tunnel. We are the warmth and the care and the compassion, as much as we carry the scars of our cruelty and anger.

This coming change is so fundamental it is a return to what is simple and essential, what is basic to life. And yet it is not easy to live. Many forces push us outwards towards complexity. These are the forces that take away our joy and demand that we work harder and harder. They drive us into conflicts we do not need and always try to obscure the simple joy of life, of being together and valuing our companionship. Fast food and mega-movies may glitter and catch our collective attention, but we know in our hearts that something fundamental is being overlooked. We do not need to drown in prosperity. Nor do we need to impose any beliefs on others. We have simply to recognize what is *real* and live this in our own lives. What is real has the energy and light to free us from so many imposed beliefs. If we allow it, this light and energy can even free us from the belief in consumerism, which feeds the greed that is destroying our planet.

In the simplicity of our human values—love, and joy, and hope—we are all connected together. But we can only discover this connection when we return to this simple core of being. Otherwise we will fall apart along with a world that has lost its center, a world that believes in its own advertising slogans. When we return to this potential of the heart, we will see what is being born, how a linking together of individuals, groups, and communities is taking place, how patterns of relationship are growing—and how life energy is flowing through these patterns. Once again humanity is recreating itself, creating a new civilization in the midst of the old.

In our focus on complexity we have overlooked the rule that the more complex something becomes, the more its energy becomes scattered and fragmented. Human beings have a unique role as the microcosm of the whole, which means that we can carry the whole multiplicity of creation within the simplicity of our essential nature. In this simplicity we carry the whole and also our divine potential and power.

When a human being is not scattered in the "ten thousand things," she is very powerful. This is a part of the purpose of spiritual practice: as we return to our essence we become more focused and able to claim our own power.

In the simple core of our being we carry the imprint of the divine in all its miraculous nature. Because "God is a simple essence," life's divinity is able to express itself more directly in our love and joy and hope and other simple qualities. Reconnecting with these qualities, we reconnect with the divine within us and with the power of the divine. When we live these qualities, we bring the power of the divine into life. This power or energy can move through the patterns of relationship that are currently being created and can flow into life. In this simple way, life can regenerate itself.

The signs of this regeneration are all around us, in the way people are coming together. The internet is an essential part of this process because it connects people regardless of the barriers of physical location, race, background, nationality, or life experience. Different people in all parts of the world are linking together, forming networks of shared interests. These networks are outside the control of any hierarchy or government. They belong to life itself.

New and diverse patterns of relationship are forming. We have yet to fully recognize that these patterns of relationship are so essential, that they are a real response to the problems and complexity of the times. They are not just for conveying information. They are creating a new, fast-changing, organic interrelationship of individuals and groups. Something is coming alive in a new way.

People are making connections on many different levels, through global trade, travel, telecommunications, conferences, and other forms of gatherings. For example, interfaith dialogues are one level of interreligious communication, while the migration of spiritual paths and traditions from the East to the West have been working at a deeper level to make a global connection, a merging of East and West, creating a light that is "neither of the East nor of the West."

We have yet to realize that this is all a part of the organism of life recreating itself on the pattern of oneness. We see these changes with the eyes of individuality and fragmentation that focus on the individual parts, still caught in the complex images of a decaying culture. The real picture is an emerging wholeness that is a life force in itself. *Life is reconnecting itself in order to survive and evolve.*

In these organic, non-hierarchical patterns of reconnection a new life force is flowing. This life force has the urgency that is needed if it is to survive and change at this time of crisis. It also has the power of oneness, and the simplicity of bringing people together. It is about sharing rather than possessiveness and isolation. It is the deep joy of knowing that we are one life. And it carries the imprint of divine oneness, which is stronger than any pattern of resistance.

PREPARING FOR THE STORM

How does the simplicity of life's new forms relate to the powerful shifts that are happening under the surface, the seismic dimension of outer changes? There is a beautiful balance in the way the organic patterns of life are complementing the changes in the depths, how human life on the surface is generating new forms to balance the inner shift.

These emerging patterns of interrelationship also serve a practical purpose. They are creating a container for new energy that is coming into life. This new life force is already surfacing through small fissures and cracks in the veneer of our civilization. It is generating new ideas, creating new ways of being.

But when new energy does not flow into new forms, it constellates into conflict, in the old patterns of duality expressed in the outbreaks of terrorism and the power dynamics of repression. What we are facing now is the emergence of a new archetypal energy, an energy that can create wonders, or take us into deeper suffering.

The archetypal world is a dimension of undifferentiated primal power. It can create great civilizations and terrible wars. An archetype that suddenly erupts into life can be devastating. Historically there have been examples of such moments, as when the wild force of Genghis Khan and his warriors destroyed the civilizations of the East. Genghis Khan constellated a powerful archetypal energy that initially manifested through violence and destruction.[3] But there are always signs that point to such dynamic shifts, signs that help humanity to go with the flow rather than resist the changes. Many families migrated west before the Mogul hoards attacked.

The danger arises when we do not notice the signs. If we are too identified with the old ways and our position or identity within them, we will miss the chance to pack up a few possessions and move on. Resisting an emerging archetype will only lead to disaster. It may appear for a few years or decades that one can hold back the tide, clinging to one's old values and images of security, but a life based on denial of the real forces at work is often haunted by a sense of unreality, as must have been experienced in the last dying days of the Roman Empire. There is also an instinctual unease, a primal insecurity, which no amount of protection can dispel.

Much of our present insecurity comes from a deep knowing that our governments and cultures are planning for a future that will never happen. They may talk about economic expansion and pension benefits, but we sense that these are just sandcastles as the tide comes in. Human beings have an instinctual wisdom deeper than our conscious minds. We know that we are being lied to, but collectively we continue with our buying and selling, knowing no other way of life—even when our dreams are pointing to a different reality:

A great storm is coming, the sky is darkening, a great wind tears the firmament apart with lightning and thunder. I wonder what is approaching. Am I watching people on a ship about to be tossed in a great sea and at the mercy of this storm?

Many people today have dreams of storms, tidal waves, and great devastation, and yet when we look around us at the shopping malls and well-stocked supermarkets, we see no cause for this fear. What do we do with our fear? What do we do with the part of us that is awakening to the possibilities and dangers that are coming?

The only response is to continue our daily life, because there is nowhere else to go, nothing else to do. In our global era there is no "safe place." This coming change will happen to the whole planet.

And yet we can be prepared; we can work to welcome the change. There is no point in stockpiling provisions or becoming self-sufficient. These are protectionist responses emanating from and perpetuating old patterns. Instead we can create a space within us so that the deep, instinctual knowing that belongs to our depths can come to the surface. We can listen to our dreams and welcome a future that we do not yet know.

Mystics are prepared for this. We are used to standing on the edge of what is known and welcoming the unknown, the unknowable. We are trained to respond from a place within us deeper than any cultural conditioning—a place that belongs to God. We try not to be imprisoned by any form or belief, and always allow our attachments to be swept aside by the greater power that comes from within. And we know that behind any apparent misfortune lie the love and laughter of the divine.

This attitude allows us to stand in the very axis of change, on the edge of the fault line, where we can help the new energy come into being. We are not frightened of devastation because we have already been destroyed by love. We are used to power greater than we can comprehend. And we know that His mercy is always greater than His justice.

In the simplicity of our ordinary selves, living our ordinary lives, with our prayers and devotions we create a container that can help humanity make this transition. We link together the inner and outer worlds so that the energy can flow more freely into the outer. And we do this not out of fear, which would contract us, but with love and joy to be of service to our Beloved, knowing that another cycle of revelation is taking place.

DIVINE DECEPTION

We each have a work to do at this time of transition, a quality of service, love, and knowledge that we can bring into life; it is written in our soul. Part of the work of reading the signs in the inner and outer life is to become awake to the real nature of our service. But distractions abound, as do illusions in the inner and outer world.

One aspect of the work of the moment is to contain the new energy of transition in our daily life. Our practices teach us not to be caught in the dramas of fear and anxiety that leave many people impotent or drive them to react through shadow dynamics. We need to have both feet on the ground because the tensions all around us are creating strange delusions in the inner and outer. Yet because the ground under our feet is shifting, there is little real security.

And the tension will only increase, creating more hope and more fear. Our work is always to stay true to the divine, to the real convictions that we carry within us. We will be tested, to see how easily we are distracted, caught in the collective dramas of gain and loss. We will be forced to confront many of our own fears and insecurities, even fears we believed long-buried or outgrown. We do not know how this energy will affect us, what patterns of resistance it will evoke. We may think that we are strong in our spiritual practice, only to discover a fragility and self-concern. Or we may discover that we are freer than we thought.

A sense of humor is vital. Laughter is often more effective than force. Recognizing how easily we get caught, we can let laughter free us. And we can carry the hope that seems to be denied to much of the collective. We believe in His oneness and we know that all is according to His will. And we live this as an affirmation of life, despite our culture's apparent darkness and the distrust that is in the air.

Many illusions will come to the surface and be blown away. One of the primal illusions to resist is that of saving the world. The lover is here in service to her Beloved. It is His world to do with as He wills. We do not know what species need to survive, just as we do not know what new species will be born. We do not know what part of our civilization needs to be destroyed and what should be redeemed. We do not know what is a relic from the past, what belongs only to this time of transition, and what is part of the future. We do not know the purpose of His creation. It is arrogance to think that we do.

The book of life is written by the hand of God, not by well-meaning people. There is laughter and infinite love in the way He tells His story, the way He reveals Himself to Himself. When we think that we are other than this process of divine revelation, we step outside of this circle into the dramas of our own creation. When we acknowledge that we do not know, we can glimpse how there is nothing other than His oneness revealing itself in a multitude of ways, in the most beautiful and terrible forms, full of divine purpose and trickery! It is always other than what we think, than what we can imagine. Awakening to this is essential to experiencing the wonder and terror of His world. *It is not about us!*

One of the first things we learn on the path is that nothing is as it appears. We realize how we are deceived and how we deceive ourselves. Life is a play of appearances in which we are caught by our own desires and projections. The path presents us with these illusions and other tricks; it deceives us. Even the idea of a path is an illusion because there is nowhere to go, no journey to make. We learn to laugh as well as cry at how we are deceived, coming to understand that everything is a fairground hall of mirrors in which we just see ourself, reflected in a myriad of different shapes. Sometimes through the cracks in our defenses we glimpse a simpler truth about ourself and life, and we can laugh with the joy of what is revealed.

On the path we come to see how we are manipulated, how we are the fool. Yet we rarely take this knowing into the wider spectrum of life, appreciating how the whole world is a deception and is itself the victim of trickery. We blame our politicians for deceiving us, for not telling us the truth. But they are children compared to the way the divine deceives us all. What is this "world stage" that seems so important? What is really being enacted?

Somehow in our Western culture we have forgotten the dimension of divine laughter. We take ourselves and our lives too seriously. This is particularly true in North America with its puritan heritage. And as our Western values spread over the earth along with Coca-Cola and McDonalds, we are forgetting that "He is the best of deceivers." It is our hubris to believe that the world must be as it appears through our eyes. We have forgotten the laughter that belongs to more "primitive" people; we become affronted when we discover we have been tricked. And because we regard ourselves and our lives so seriously, we have lost the quality of cunning that can help us find our way through this hall of mirrors.

The ancient Greeks had a word for this quality of cunning: *metis*.[4] *Metis* was essential for sailors who needed to find their way through uncharted waters, and also for those who journeyed inward into the underworld. The forefathers of our Western culture regarded *metis* as a vital means for finding one's way in the unknown and the dark, for discovering the truth in a world of deception. We see cunning as a negative quality, as a means by which we cheat and are cheated. But if the whole world is a play of appearances, how can we know what is real without cunning?

If everything is a deception, what are we to believe? On the mystical path we often realize that what we thought were our own deepest convictions are just another layer of self-deception, protecting us from what is real. We relearn the simplest things. We learn how to breathe; we learn that "when we are hungry we eat, when we are tired we sleep." We learn to laugh at ourselves and our lives. And in the silence, amidst all of the clamor and clutter of life, we offer ourself to Him whom we love. This thread of simplicity runs through all of life's deceptions. It is our deepest human nature and carries an imprint of His name. It will guide us through life's deceptions because it belongs to the Creator and not the myriad mirrors of His creation.

But we need cunning to find this thread, what the Sufis call "catching the hint." We need to be fully awake to the moment and to be aware of both the seen and the unseen, the outer and the inner. Then it becomes apparent how "We shall show them Our signs on the horizons and in themselves, until it is clear to them that He is the Real." (*sura* 41:53)

FORCES OF TRANSFORMATION

That we live in unsure times is not just a cliché. Forces that have not been in our world for millennia are now present. Some of these forces, specifically oriented towards change and transformation, are here to help in this transition; the forces behind the changes in technology, science, and other areas that we will need for our future are some examples.

Other forces are creating the foundations of the new age, working deep in the unconscious, constellating archetypal and spiritual patterns that will form the basis for the values and beliefs of the future, creating the sacred and healing symbols of the coming age. Still other forces are designed to disturb and destroy the present structures, those that belong to our hierarchical, patriarchal culture. Although these forces are necessary to clear away the past, they are less apparently beneficial and bring an energy of chaos and destruction.

Mostly we are unconscious of these forces; we feel their effects without knowing their true origin. We sense that something is changing, but often we react out of our fear or insecurity. Or we may become over-enthusiastic and in our excitement lose our center. Our groundlessness leaves us ineffective, and only makes matters worse.

We need both common sense and *metis* to guide us. We also need to acknowledge that something is happening beyond our control. One of the features of our patriarchal culture is a desire to control our inner and outer worlds, and as a result we are fearful of what we cannot control. We are terrified of chaos, although anyone who has experienced real transformation knows that chaos is a necessary ingredient of true creativity. Without an element of chaos life stagnates.

Amidst these powerful forces that are reconstellating our life there are other, more minor energies awaking. They have a magical quality, and while some are beneficial, others are mischievous, not abiding by the rules of the status quo. They are a foretaste of the coming era when life's magical nature will resurface, as many of the barriers that separate the inner and outer worlds will fall away or be dissolved. We have forgotten or dismissed the magical nature of creation, but gradually the blinkers that have shielded us from this dimension of life will be removed.[5] We will find that our rational perception is quite inadequate to explain what is happening, and we will discover that we are part of a world full of delight and mischief.

Forces belonging to another dimension are also affecting us. These are forces that relate to our place within the cosmos. The evolutionary shift that is taking place concerns not just our planet in isolation. We are a part of an immense pattern of interrelated energies we call our galaxy. As we step into an awareness of oneness and the interrelationship of all of life here in this world, our perspective will begin to include the cosmos as a whole.

How these cosmic forces affect us is unknown, as it has been many millennia since we have experienced the direct impact of such transformative, evolutionary energies. But patterns of relationship are being created that stretch far beyond our individual planet.

Other forces are also present at this time, powers of light and darkness that originate far beyond our world. They do not belong to the play of opposites, and yet can affect our world in positive and negative ways.

These energies and others that are impacting us exist on different levels, reflecting the multidimensional nature of life and the vaster cosmos in which we exist. Spiritual masters and their disciples are working with these energies. The different spiritual centers contained within the heart embrace all the different levels of existence, and the higher consciousness of a spiritual master can work with energies on the different levels, balancing and aligning them with our collective destiny and with the energy patterns in the earth. The divine consciousness of the heart also works to remind these different energies and their sources of the oneness of which they are an expression, and of the fact that each energy is a witness to divine oneness.

An awareness of oneness is central to our present evolution, and through the awakened heart of His servant this awareness can be given to the different energies coming into our world. The forces erupting from the depths can be given the ingredient of human consciousness aligned with the will of the Creator witnessing His oneness. This brings these energies together in a new way, a way that welcomes the future and enables all the different forces to work together in harmony, forming a multidimensional mandala-like pattern of wholeness. Through the heart these energies are imprinted with the divine purpose that is unfolding: the awakening of the whole world to a new level of awareness.

THE RELATIONSHIP
BETWEEN THE WORLDS

*The light of the body is the eye:
if therefore thine eye be single,
thy whole body shall be full of light.*

Matthew 6:22

THE WORLD OF GOD'S COMMAND AND
THE WORLD OF CREATION

What is the relationship between the higher spiritual
centers within the human being—the world of God's
command (*'âlâm-e amr*)—and the world we experience
through the senses and the veils of the ego—the world
of creation (*'âlâm-e kalq*)?[1]

The world of God's command is quite different from
the world of creation. The world of creation, which belongs
to the *nafs* and the four elements, is governed by the laws
of cause and effect, action and reaction. It is a world of
appearances and deception in which things rarely are as
they appear, as we each discover as we make the painful
transition from innocence to experience. The ego appears
to be the ruler, rather than the Self, the real king.

Our energy centers in the world of creation belong
to our survival instinct with its forces of fear and aggression, to our sexual drive, which pulls us into the drama of

desires, and to the drive for domination, which belongs to the will of the ego.[2] The drive for domination is also associated with providing for personal needs: food, clothing, and shelter. This world often seems dominated by will, while love, the most powerful force in creation, sadly appears hidden. It is easy to say "this is just the veil of appearances," but it is within this veil that most of us live.

In contrast, the world of God's command is ruled by divine decree rather than man's ambition. Love is the dominant force, and in its light there is no deception. There are no shadows in which deceptions can be born, no dance of appearances: we are seen as we really are and everything is known according to its true nature—"For now we see through a glass, darkly; but then face to face; now I know in part; but then I shall know even as also I am known."[3]

The world of God's command is a radiant, ever-expanding dimension of light upon light, a deepening immersion in divine oneness that leads to the complete absorption of the individual in the most hidden Reality that is found in the innermost chamber of the heart (*akhfâ*). This is a Reality that permeates all of creation, all of existence and non-existence, and yet is veiled from any perception of consciousness. It is the simplest essence of life and also the greatest secret.

In this world there is real harmony, and the peace that belongs to the soul. There are different degrees of divine light, greater depths of revelation, as suggested by the different spiritual centers, the *latâ'if*,[4] but it is all governed by truth, openness, and honesty.

Traditionally, the wayfarer aspires to awaken to the world of God's command and to be free from bondage to the world of creation—to the ego and its desires in the world of the senses. The awakening of the spiritual

centers within the individual, and the work of purification
that precedes this awakening, are part of the process of
liberation that belongs to the journey of spiritual ascent.
This journey involves the transformation of a human
being from imprisonment in the world of matter to the
realization of union with God and our true nature as
divine light.

Yet many wayfarers who have made the journey tell
us that we are always united. What they discover is that
the image of the journey and of any separation between
the worlds is an illusion. Nothing is higher or lower. All
is One: "He is the existent and the non-existent"; "there
is no other and there is no existence other than He."
The simplicity of this realization is so immense because
everything is included. The darkness is His darkness
and the light His light. This is not theory but a mystical
realization.

Grounded in this realization, the mystic is a part of
creation *as it really is*. And with this awareness, the relationship between the world of God's command and the
world of creation takes on a very different perspective.

Once we realize that *everything* is an aspect of the
divine, the world of creation fulfills its divine purpose,
just as the world of God's command fulfills its purpose.
It is only through the combination of the two worlds
that His hidden self can become known, His unity be
perceived in multiplicity. Then the world becomes a
place of divine revelation:

> If the spirit had not attained its various means
> of perception through attachment to the bodily
> frame and acquired various instruments, talents
> and faculties for perceiving the unseen and the
> seen, it would never have reached this station in
> the knowledge of the Unity of the Essence and the

attributes of the Knower of the Unseen and Seen. Since the angels did not have the characteristics and attributes acquired by the human spirit when it was attached to the frame, they were unfit for the task of viceregency and deputyship, unable to bear the burden of Trust, and incapable of being a mirror for the beauty and splendour of God. None would ever have discovered the treasure of "I was a hidden treasure."[5]

Awakening to the light of our higher nature helps us find our way in the world of creation. The light within the heart is the guide that liberates us, first helping us to see our faults and the hindrances that block us, then pointing out the path we need to follow. The light of the heart helps to show us our real destiny, which is often quite different from what we imagine. It helps to awaken us more fully to our real potential and the way we can be of service. Through this inner light, we are able to see this world as it really is, no longer blinded or blinkered by the desires of the ego. We come to recognize His signs and to witness His oneness. We come alive to the presence of God in the inner and outer worlds.

The mystic brings together the worlds of the unseen and the seen, "seeing all things as proofs of divine unity" and "seeing God's outwardness in all things." The inner worlds are no longer a place to escape from the bondage of this world, but a quality of light, or awareness, that He needs in His world in order to reveal Himself to Himself. The way that the darkness of the world hides the divine light, its play of shadows, desires, and ignorance, is a revelation as unique as the way the inner worlds appear to reveal His light. Both worlds are in service to the wonder of His creation: helping us to see His face in His world.

INTERPENETRATING WORLDS

In the past era mystical consciousness developed a profound understanding of the inner worlds, experiencing dimensions of light and absorption in God (or for Buddhist mystics, nirvana). These inner realities were often experienced as quite separate from experiences of the outer world, and many mystics lived in monasteries or caves, isolated from the demands of life. Even in Sufism, which is not a monastic path, the emphasis was on turning away from the outer world to discover the inner truth within the heart. This inner orientation belonged to an era that stressed a transcendent divinity, often at the expense of the immanent qualities of the divine—particularly those that belong to the feminine and the physical world.

As we enter a new era, we are noticing a shift towards including everyday life and the physical world in spiritual practice. In the West many people who are attracted to spiritual life are unable or unwilling to embrace the life of a renunciate. Monasticism has lost its appeal. Is this a cultural trend, a lack of serious spiritual commitment in our Western world? Is the grip of materialism so strong that we cannot leave behind our worldly attachments?

Or could this shift be part of a new pattern of spiritual awareness that does not seek to separate the inner and outer, the spiritual and worldly? Perhaps we are moving towards an awareness of oneness that embraces all of life, the light and the dark, the world of God's command and the world of creation.

We have forgotten that "He never reveals Himself in the same form twice." As the patterns of revelation change, so does the work of the wayfarer, the way we work to reveal His light within ourself and the world. The trends we are experiencing as a spiritual collective are signs of a new revelation of the divine. Once we give up the notion that the individual is separate from the whole and instead see the light of the seeker as part of the light of the world, then we begin to recognize the profound change that is taking place. We will come to see how the world of God's command interpenetrates the world of creation, how they are not two separate dimensions, but different facets of a oneness that continually reveals and hides itself.

Those who have made the journey into the heart of hearts know the love that is at the core of life, the love that gives meaning and magic to every breath. One of the paradoxes of life is that the inner reality of light and love is present all around us, in every breath we breathe, and yet it is hidden, veiled by the ego. It is the real substance of life, the inner secret of creation. It is our natural self which we have forgotten, the paradise from which we have been banished, where we walked naked in the presence of God.

Why should this simple truth remain hidden? Does humanity have to remain exiled from its own essential nature? Or can we reclaim this paradise, this simple and joyful sense of what is real, amidst the demands of everyday life? Then we might begin to see that the worlds do not have to appear separate, and the reality of light can be present even in the shadows of the world of creation.

The traditional response is that this dimension of light and love is only accessible to those who have renounced the ego and purified their lower nature. If the *nafs* imprisons us in the world of creation, then we have to leave it behind. But does this mean that the doors of revelation are only open to a few, and the world as a whole must remain shrouded in darkness, a wasteland dying from humanity's greed and forgetfulness?

Life needs the light of the world of God's command; it needs this love and power to purify and protect it. The wayfarer knows that only in the light of what is real can we find our way, can we reclaim the source of life: "For with Thee is the fountain of life: in Thy light shall we see light."[6]

The work of the mystic is to bring this light into life. With our help, the light of His love can awaken in the midst of our present collective patterns; it can begin to redeem our world and help restore the joy, beauty, and wonder that have been lost.

BEYOND A PARADIGM OF OPPOSITES

Does the paradigm of opposites really hold up if we look at it closely? There are the primal opposites of night and day, life and death: but how often is the nighttime completely dark, the day without shadows? Life and death are part of each other, part of the continual flow of creation, and each moment we die and each moment we are born. Transformation is both a death and a birth, and in the real wholeness of a human being we realize how the many parts of ourself come together.

The newly awakening oneness does not reveal itself through contrasting pairs of opposites but through patterns of relationship, relationships built upon similarities rather than opposition. Once we clear away the paradigm of opposition, we will encounter a very different picture of a life that is multihued, with each color expressing a different aspect of divine beauty. If our eyes are open, we can see this global shift around us in our city streets with all the different peoples, the mixture of races, with all the different music that is being played, the different customs and religions: so many ways to worship the One.

Something has changed that is fundamental, and yet we overlook it, or choose to ignore what it means. Despite our political systems, fundamentalist religions, or racial ideologies, the world is no longer a place we can divide into opposites.

The old ways remain present; the dynamics of duality will take decades to die. But the secret is to look to what is being born. The emerging patterns of relationship carry the new energy of life, the energy that is coming into being and will transform our planet.

Furthermore, the light of what is real cannot follow the old ways—it cannot be constellated into dualism. In order to be brought into life, it needs the participation of individuals aligned to these emerging patterns, whose consciousness has been awakened to the dynamics of oneness. It is through groups of individuals (groups that relate in a non-hierarchical way) that the light of the Real can flow where it is needed, can come from the inner into the outer, from the world of God's command into the world of creation.

The alignment between the inner and outer worlds has already been made. Connections have been made out of a very fine substance that can bring the light of the Real to the edge of the outer worlds. This has been given to humanity by the masters who guide the destiny of our planet. But it is for humanity to bring this light into the midst of life. This is our responsibility. The light needs the density of our created self, our *nafs* and lower nature, in order to become present in life. It needs the "redness" of our blood to live in this world. It needs to be "earthed" through our density and darkness, through our ordinary self. Otherwise its potential for real change will remain just a possibility, and our world will not be transformed.

Life is recreating itself through us. The life force working through us is uncovering patterns of relationship that belong to wholeness, that belong to life systems founded upon interrelationship and interdependence. We know how these patterns form the ecological basis of life. In the past centuries we have focused on "the survival of the fittest" and all of the dynamics of competition that relate to this perspective. And life does have forces of aggression, domination, and competition. But these are a part of a deeper wholeness in which all forms of life exist together. Now we need to consciously reclaim this deeper pattern, recognize the ways life-forms and different peoples can interrelate and nourish each other—for example, the way in the last decades that the East has nourished the West with its deeper spiritual knowledge, and the way the West has generated new ideas and technologies that can help the "less developed" parts of the world.

This may seem a simplistic approach to the many problems of the present, and we have witnessed how the energy of globalism can seem to get highjacked by the forces of competition and greed, how it has also brought terrorism to our doorstep. We cannot avoid these shadow dynamics; the danger comes when our reactions just reinforce protectionism and the images of duality, "us" and "them." Sadly, it is these darker images that attract the attention of our media and create collective anxiety.

But this is really a distraction from the real need of the moment: life is recreating itself on a global level and it needs our participation. We cannot afford to be caught in the images of the past; if we are, we will miss the opportunity and remain part of what is dying rather than the new life.

If we are present in the moment, we will naturally find ourself aligned with the emerging patterns of life: life will speak to us in our own way because we are a part of life. Despite our patterns of resistance, life will align us with what is needed. If we try to create our future or hold onto the past, we will remain stuck in the images of what is dying. But as most spiritual disciplines teach us, only by being present can we be awake to what is real: only in the present moment can we participate in what is really happening and not just perpetuate the images of our fears and desires.

In the present moment we can discover how the inner and outer have been aligned and are waiting for us to make the connection. We *are* that connection, the link between the worlds, the place where the light comes from the inner to the outer, from the world of God's command to the world of creation. We are both the higher and the lower, and we are the oneness that embraces both. When these two realities come together, they start to spin, to move together in a way quite different from the dynamics of dualism. Through their union something new can be born, a way of being that *is the future*. This is what is waiting to happen. From the two will be born a third that is "neither of the East nor of the West." Through this awakening, the individual will begin to realize her real potential as the microcosm of the whole, and as a part of an interrelated web of life and light. This is the next level of realization of individual consciousness.

THE LIGHT OF THE WORLD

The world of God's command is not separate from the world of creation. Without its higher spiritual centers, the world of creation would be a pale shadow of itself, and it would not be a place of divine revelation. Without the dense planes of manifestation, there would be nothing to reflect the pure light, and He would remain in His inward essence. In the wonder of His multiplicity, in His many forms, He becomes known to Himself. It is the light of the higher worlds reflected in the lower worlds that makes this possible. The purpose of our incarnation is to help in this work: to bring the light of the higher into the outer world so that His face can become visible, His glory and majesty become known, not just to the initiate, but to all of life.

When a soul is born, it brings with it its pure light. This is one of the reasons that there is such joy in the birth of a child: we recognize in it life's divine nature. Through the eyes of the child for an instant we see life as it really is. In the memory of humanity lives a time when we all lived in this paradise, in the simple joy of being alive, when the light of our spiritual self was not hidden. It is sometimes called "The Golden Age." But just as the developing ego of the child veils it from the light of what is real, so did the gift of individual consciousness force us from paradise. We still carry the scars of that apparent abandonment.

Since the Golden Age, eras have come and gone. The most recent era has witnessed the development over centuries of a powerful focus on a masculine, transcendent divinity, which has emphasized the separation between the worlds. This has had a very real effect, not only in forming the image of a spiritual journey away from the world, but also in creating a denser veil between the world of creation and the higher spiritual centers, a veil that exists both within the individual and in the world. This veil has become almost impenetrable over the past centuries, partly due to our rational culture and our pursuit of materialism.

The density of the veil makes it more difficult for the light of the inner worlds to be seen in the outer world, and for the love of the inner to nourish the outer. We know how hard we have to struggle to reclaim the light of our true nature. We are less aware of how the world itself has been separated from its source in the inner: it too has been starved of a certain spiritual nourishment.

Just as we need the light of our higher nature to find our way, so does the world need this light to awaken to its true purpose. Our imprisonment of the world in dense clouds of materialism and forgetfulness has deprived it of its magical nature. The magical nature of creation is essential to its survival and transformation.

The light from the world of God's command can awaken the magical nature of life, just as it awakens an individual to the miraculous world in which we really live. In the light of His love we can see and participate in His world, which is a dynamic, spiritual being full of the wondrous and unexpected. Without this light we see only the world of our senses, a world we have raped and made destitute and left clinging to the edge of its survival. We see a world defined by our ego and its desires, rather than a place of unlimited possibilities that belongs to God.

We remain attached to our limited perception of life because we have imagined a world that we can control. The past era has taken us down this road of domination. Even the Catholic church focused on worldly power rather than spiritual awareness, consolidating its power through persecuting the Gnostics and other mystics, burning women who had healing powers, and suppressing many of the esoteric teachings of Christ. What did not adhere to its hierarchy was tortured as heretical.

We remain frightened of the unknown, yet the divine is the greatest unknown. In banishing God to heaven, we have created the illusion of being in power on earth. The developments of science have worked to enhance the illusion, describing a world we could master with reason and technology. If we welcome the divine back into the earth, into the midst of everyday life, we will no longer be able to dominate by force and will, to sustain the illusion of control. We will have to recognize a greater power that is not just in heaven but present in life.

THE POWER OF MATTER

As we move into a consciousness of oneness, we will no longer be able to reject or neglect the lower in favor of the higher. Our conscious attention will be drawn deep into the darkness of the earth, of the material world. The true nature of matter, in all its mystery and magic, will begin to reveal itself.

In the past era of dualism the seeker often used his aspiration to escape the darkness of the world, to become free of the physical limitations of matter. Journeying within, he discovered worlds of light without these limitations. But now we need to reclaim the deeper meaning of matter, experience the revelations of creation.[7]

In the darkness of this world there is a divine power which men have feared because it belongs to the wisdom of the feminine. Much of our Western spiritual drive to become free from the bondage of matter and realize a transcendent spirituality can be linked with this fear, which the masculine has dogmatized into a battle of spirit against matter. St. Paul, not Jesus, spoke about the battle of the "Spirit against the flesh,"[8] which later became part of the Church's masculine ideology.

The feminine has deep understanding of the power of matter. Women carry the instinctual knowing of the divine substance in matter and of how to bring this substance into life, because this knowledge is fundamental in the process of giving birth, in bringing a soul into human form. Now this wisdom is needed for the regeneration of the earth, for the earth's awakening.

The feminine knows that what appears to be a constriction and limitation is actually a place of trans-formation: the earth is the womb of our rebirth. This is reflected in the ancient teaching that the soul can only realize divine truth while in the body. Specifically, one needs the *kundalini* energy, which is an earth energy, in order to reach Reality.[9] The world of matter may appear to deny us our spiritual nature, to cover it in darkness and desire. But matter has a divine energy that is necessary for the soul to fully realize its divine nature.[10]

What is true for the individual is also true for the whole world. There is a power in the earth that is central to our collective evolution, to the awakening of the soul of the world. This is the secret substance of creation that was known by some of the Gnostics, who worked to liberate its energy. One of the Gnostic teachings is that through his crucifixion, Christ, the awakener, liberated the light within matter for the whole world. The church repressed the Gnostic teachings, but the knowledge remained in the alchemical tradition, which—rather than seeking the light in the heavens—looked for it in the darkness of the *prima materia*, the undifferentiated primal matter of creation.

In our inner journey we realize that we are our own alchemist, transforming the darkness of our psyche into gold, discovering the light hidden in the *prima materia* of our shadow and instinctual nature. In our darkness lie a knowing and also an energy that are necessary for our journey:

> The inner journey takes us into the depths of our own being where the primal power of the Self exists as undifferentiated energy. We need this

energy for the work; we need the power of our
natural being in order to be ourself and live true
to this unconditioned self.[11]

Without the power of our "natural being" there
can be no transformation. We also need the wisdom
and self-knowledge that come from sincere self-inquiry,
from exploring our darkness. The statement of Christ,
"Be ye therefore wise as serpents,"[12] points to this quality
of wisdom.

Essential to this inner work is accepting the darkness
as it is. Only when it is accepted without judgment does our
darkness transform and reveal its hidden nature, become
the gold it always was. The alchemists understood that
the real transformation is the transformation of consciousness, which enables us to recognize and then work with
the light that is always present in the darkness.

Working within ourselves, we are also working with
the whole. The individual is the microcosm of the whole.
Through our instinctual self we connect with all of life.
This is one reason why the *nafs* is so important: it gives
us access to the world of creation and enables us to reveal
the light hidden in the earth. Through our higher centers
we connect with inner dimensions of light; through our
lower centers we are part of the created world and can
access its secrets.

The light hidden in creation has a different quality
from the light of the world of God's command. This light,
called by the alchemists the *lumen naturae*, reveals many
of the secrets of creation, including its magical nature.[13]
We need to be able to work with the light hidden in matter, just as we have learned to work with the light of our
higher spiritual centers. Finally, we need to bring the two
lights together so that a third light can be born. In this

new light we will be able to see and fully participate in a new revelation: a new understanding of what it means to be a human being.

THE UNIQUENESS OF THE PATH

How can we help awaken the light in the darkness, the hidden magic of matter? How can we play our part in this coming together of the higher and lower?

From the perspective of oneness, we can recognize that the world of light needs this world of creation in order to reveal itself. Without this dimension of shadows there can be no revelation. The different worlds are inter-penetrating, interdependent dimensions which together reveal the One. Even to see it in terms of opposites coming together just continues the paradigm of duality.

Just as the lower needs the higher, the higher also needs the lower. What matters is how *we* relate to this unfolding, interdependent oneness. Do we stay within the attitudes of the past, seeking only to ascend, or do we recognize the potency of darkness and density and become receptive to its magic? Do we dare to appreciate the true wonder of the world of creation? All is He, but we are needed to become aware of the meaning of this oneness: how the worlds of creation and of God's command *together* reveal His secret.

We each contribute something different, unique to our own specific destiny. "Take thyself for a light," said the Buddha to his disciple, Ananda. The path is created with each step we take; it is our own willingness to let go of the old and welcome the light of the new that will reveal what is needed from us.

We can recognize how our instinctual drives and ego desires veil us from the light of the Self—how they keep us imprisoned in cycles of self-gratification rather than witnessing His revelation, how they deny us our divine nature and help create the fog of forgetfulness that isolates us within the self-created world of the ego. And yet our instinctual drives, the forces of self-preservation, are necessary for our life in this world. They are what weaves us into the web of life, the interconnectedness of creation. And it is in the depths of our instinctual self that we discover the *lumen naturae*, the light hidden in the darkness. Here we reclaim the wisdom of our natural self.

Because He gave us free will, we have the freedom to live the will of the ego and not our higher will. In order to fully access our higher nature, we need to surrender, to allow the ego to "die." But we need to do it in the context of our lives. We need to recognize that a spiritual "ascent" that focuses on what we imagine is our higher nature and denies our darkness might simply be an attempt to escape from the difficulties and demands of everyday life. The correct balance of the higher and lower, spiritual discrimination, is one of the most difficult spiritual qualities to develop. Living in both worlds requires constant attention—and a sense of humor, because it is never what one expects!

Living this willingness, awareness, and laughter is different for everyone. One seeker might find she is offered a job on Wall Street after months of inner work—an opportunity to ground spiritual understanding in the density of the business world and open pathways of light through patterns of greed. For another, having a family might be a way for inner qualities of love and attention to enter the outer through the instinctual relationship of mother and child. Every day is a new opportunity to live

this awareness in the inner and outer worlds, to participate in the revelation of life's secret. In many different
ways life opens us to its hidden nature. One friend was
given an understanding about the mystery of light within
matter in the energy of her body:

> In a dream I was shown all the cells, all the *chakras*
> of the body. In each there was a little bag like a
> flexible pouch, containing golden oil. When a
> certain ignition or initiating event occurred in life,
> the pouch in each cell contracted and squeezed
> out some oil, which then flamed up with this
> light-substance. It was like light upon light.

This is a new era, and that which is new has little
precedent. Our work is to stay attuned to what we feel
in the moment, to allow our resistances to fall away, to
welcome the unknown. Perhaps we will have a sense of
what is happening only after a step has been taken, when
the mystery of the unseen becomes an outer reality. The
thirteenth-century Sufi, Najm al-Dîn Razî, describes this
possibility:

> For in the beginning the spirit had knowledge
> of universals and not of the particulars; it had
> knowledge of the world of the unseen and not of
> the manifest. When it was joined to this world and
> duly trained and nurtured, it acquired knowledge
> of both universals and particulars, and became
> "knower of the unseen and the manifest" as God's
> viceregent.[14]

It can help to know that life is following a natural
course, that the divine has its own momentum. The light
of the higher is coming into the lower, helping to release

the light that belongs to the world of creation, and it is up to us to work with what is *already happening*—to let go of the blocks and resistance that inhibit this natural course.

Energy follows consciousness. Through our daily life, attention, and practices, through the breath, we participate in this process. And it is nothing special—it is the most ordinary, which is why it is so often overlooked. Through our inner acceptance of the ordinary, the light of the higher flows into the lower. Through our participation it happens. It is a way of life rather than a spiritual practice.

We can ask ourselves, are we still looking for something "other," something transcendent? Or are we seeing what is, and recognizing that it is part of a whole in which everything is connected together? This simple awareness about everyday life is a profound realization. It is like the fish recognizing water, or the wayfarer becoming aware of the real miracle of the breath.

The particulars of the path are the particulars of our life. But we must also see that each particular is universal, an expression of oneness. It is all one breath, breathed in many different ways in each moment. We are the breath of the One. We are the multiplicity and also the oneness. The wonder is the many ways in which the oneness manifests, each unique, each a different expression of the one, all connected together, all interrelated. And we are a part of this divine consciousness, awaking to its wonder.

ANIMA MUNDI

AWAKENING THE SOUL OF THE WORLD

God redeems humanity, but nature needs
to be redeemed by human alchemists, who are
able to induce the process of transformation,
which alone is capable of liberating the
light imprisoned in physical creation.

Stephan Hoeller[1]

The world is a living spiritual being. This was understood by the ancient philosophers and the alchemists
who referred to the spiritual essence of the world as the
anima mundi, the "Soul of the World." They regarded the
World Soul as a pure ethereal spirit diffused throughout
all nature, the divine essence that embraces and energizes
all life in the universe.

Throughout history our understanding of the world
as a living being with a spiritual essence has dramatically
changed. Plato understood that "the cosmos is a single
Living Creature which contains all living creatures within
it."[2] While this tradition was carried on by the Gnostics
and later the alchemists, the church fathers imaged a
world that was neither divine nor sacred. A transcendent
divinity was the source of all creation, and humanity lived
in exile from heaven in a state of sin. This doctrine created a split between matter and spirit, causing the world
to be seen as separate from its creator.

The understanding of the world as sacred resurfaced from time to time over the next centuries. In the Gothic movement of the twelfth century, and later in the Renaissance, the created world was briefly seen through the image of the World Soul. In their cathedrals the Gothic architects reflected their vision of a sacred order within creation that belongs to this feminine divine principle. The World Soul animated and formed nature according to divine proportions, which the architects, masons, sculptors, and stained-glass artists imaged in their creations.[3]

Again during the Renaissance nature was briefly seen as a living spiritual essence:

> If medieval theology had removed God to a wholly transcendent sphere, to the Renaissance Platonists nature was permeated by life, divinity, and numinous mystery, a vital expression of the World Soul and the living powers of creation. In the words of Richard Tarnas, "The garden of the world was again enchanted, with magical powers and transcendent meaning implicit in every part of nature."[4]

In the Renaissance the World Soul was understood as a spiritual essence within creation, guiding the unfolding of life and the cosmos. In the words of the Renaissance philosopher Giordano Bruno, the World Soul "illumines the universe and directs nature in producing her species in the right way."[5] The World Soul was also the creative principle that the Renaissance artists sought to channel in their work. Their art was based upon the same sacred proportions they saw in nature, and they understood the imagination as a magical power that can "lure and channel the energies of the *anima mundi.*"

The Renaissance left us great wonders of art and the imagination. It was a brief flowering, however. The orthodoxies of the church re-established the split between matter and spirit, and the rise of science began to image the natural world as a machine whose disembodied workings human beings could rationally understand and master. The magical world of creative mystery infused with divine spirit became a dream belonging only to poets and the laboratories and symbolic writings of the alchemists.

The alchemists continued to explore the *anima mundi*. While the church looked for light in the heavens, the alchemists sought the light hidden in matter. They understood that there was a sacred essence in the fabric of creation, which through their experiments and imagination they worked to release. For the alchemists the *anima mundi* is the divine spark in matter, the "philosophical Mercury," which is the "universal and scintillating fire in the light of nature, which carries the heavenly spirit with it."

Alchemy is concerned with turning lead into gold, liberating the light hidden in the darkness—"the fiery sparks of the world soul, i.e. the light of nature... dispersed or sprinkled throughout the structure of the great world into all fruits of the elements everywhere."[6] The alchemists also understood that there is a connection between the *anima mundi* and the soul or innermost secret of man. The source of the wisdom and knowledge of the all-pervading essence of the *anima mundi* was "the innermost and most secret *numinosum* of man."[7]

In the last century Carl Jung rediscovered the wisdom of the alchemical *opus* and showed how alchemical symbols image the process of inner transformation that can release this hidden light. Jung differentiated between two forms of spiritual light: *lumen dei*, the light proceeding from the spiritual realm of a transcendent God, and *lumen naturae*, the light hidden in matter and the forces of nature. The Divine Light may be experienced through revelation and spiritual practices that give us access to our transcendent Self. The Light of Nature needs to be released through inner alchemy so that it can work creatively in the world.

The tradition of alchemy reinterpreted into the language of inner transformation is a key to help us to liberate our natural light and to transform the world. The alchemical light hidden in darkness is our own light, which is also the divine spark within matter. Our natural light is part of the light of the World Soul. This alchemical unlocking of matter can be associated with freeing, or awakening, the World Soul, the *anima mundi*. As a microcosm of the whole, the individual can participate directly in the alchemical process that liberates this light, a light that is needed to understand the mysteries of creation and the ways of working with its magical nature. With the *lumen naturae* we can once again learn how to unlock the secrets of nature, so that we no longer have to attack and destroy the natural world in order to survive.

Alchemy is our Western tradition of inner transformation. Sufis have always known about the inner process of alchemy.[8] One of the early Sufi masters, Dhû-l-Nûn, was described as an alchemist, and a great twelfth-century Sufi, al-Ghazzâlî, titled one of his most important books *The Alchemy of Happiness*. Sufis have mastered the alchemy of the heart, through which the energy of love transforms the individual to reveal the light hidden within the darkness of the *nafs* or lower self. They developed a detailed science (described in the following chapter, "The Light of the Heart") for working with the chambers of the heart to effect an inner transformation that gives the wayfarer access to the light of his true nature. This work does not belong just to the individual, but can have a direct relationship to the whole of creation and the heart of the world. Once we recognize the mysterious connection between our own innermost essence and the Soul of the World, we can use the tools of inner transformation to work directly with the Soul of the World, to help the *anima mundi* reveal its divine light and awaken.

AS ABOVE SO BELOW

As a result of Jung's writings on alchemy, we have begun to understand the nature of the inner alchemical work. The work on the alchemical lead—the *prima materia*, that which is "glorious and vile, precious and of small account and is found everywhere"[9]—is the work on the *shadow*, the rejected and unacknowledged parts of our psyche. The philosopher's stone, the gold made from the lead, is our own true nature, the Self. Rather than a transcendent, disembodied divinity, alchemy reveals a divine light that exists in the very depths of our psyche. This light hidden in darkness, the *lumen naturae*, is also our instinctual self and natural way of being, which until it is revealed is covered over by patterns of conditioning and the layers of the false self.

What is the difference between the light discovered in the depths of the psyche and the light of our transcendent divine Self glimpsed in meditation or other experiences? *It is the same light* experienced in different ways. The Sufis know that the Beloved, the source of all light, has both an immanent and a transcendent quality. He whom we love is both "nearer to him than his

jugular vein" and "beyond even his idea of the beyond."
The Self, "larger than large and smaller than small," has
the same dual quality.

The yogi deep in meditation and the alchemist in
his laboratory are seeking the same light, the same divine
nature. Everything that we experience has a dual nature,
a masculine and a feminine aspect, and the same is true
of the light of the Self. It can be experienced in its masculine form as a pure transcendent light, consciousness
without the constrictions of the psyche or the physical
world. In meditation we can first glimpse and then rest
in our eternal and infinite nature, and come to know
a reality not defined or constricted by our body or the
manifest world. This is a reality of light upon light, our
colorless and formless essence.

We can also come to know our divine nature in its
feminine, embodied nature, as the light of being, our
natural wisdom, the gold of our true nature. In this light
we experience and know the divine within creation, the
way our Beloved reveals Himself in a multitude of forms,
each form a different expression of His infinite being. We
see how each color, each smell, every taste, even every
thought and feeling, is a unique expression of the divine.
In this way we come to know Him in His creation in a
way that is hidden in the transcendent. In this revelation we see that each thing is unique and that all things
are one, and we discover the relationship of the parts to
the whole—the interconnected wonder of creation. We
see the rich tapestry of life and know that it is one Being
revealing Itself in so many ways.

If we are not to remain in the paradigm of duality,
living our inherited split between masculine and feminine,
spirit and matter, we need to acknowledge both of these
aspects. We cannot afford to follow the footsteps of the
patriarchal church fathers and seek only a transcendent

light, look only towards heaven. We also need to know the light hidden in matter and understand the magic of creation that it reveals. We need to know the mysteries of creation as celebrated in the most sacred text of the alchemists, the *Emerald Tablet*, attributed to Hermes Trismegistos:

> What is below is like that which is above, and what is above is like that which is below, to accomplish the miracles of the one thing.[10]

The light hidden in matter is the one light experienced within the mystery of creation, the hidden treasure revealed through the dance of multiplicity. The creation of the manifest world is a revelation of the hidden nature of the divine, as expressed in the *hadith*, "I was a hidden treasure and I longed to be known, so I created the world." But we can only experience the wonder and know the true nature of this revelation through the light hidden within it. Just as He has hidden His secret within us—"Man is My secret and I am his secret"—so has He hidden Himself within His creation. Sometimes, in moments amidst the beauty or glory of nature, in the vastness of the stars or the perfection of the early morning dew on a flower, we glimpse this wonder. The light hidden in matter breaks through and we stand in awe before our Creator, as reflected in the words of the poet Gerard Manley Hopkins:

> The world is charged with the grandeur of God.
> It will flame out, like shining from shook foil.[11]

Through this light we can awaken to the divine nature of life and experience the real beauty of His revelation. There is only one light—"as above so below"—and yet the *lumen naturae* has a different quality to the *lumen dei*, allowing a different quality of revelation. In His creation He reveals Himself in a way that is not revealed by His transcendent light, the *lumen dei*. What is true for the Creator is also true for us who are "made in His image." The light that is discovered in the depths of the psyche, through the work on the shadow and the inner alchemical *opus*, reveals part of our divine nature that is hidden from a purely transcendent consciousness. We come to know ourself and our Beloved in a new way. For each of us this revelation is unique. Part of the wonder of creation is how she offers a different experience to each of us; even the same apple tasted by two people will be a different experience. Through His light we can see life as it really is, in the uniqueness of our own experience of it and not just through the veils of our projections, and so taste the divine uniqueness of each moment. At the same time we experience this uniqueness as part of a greater oneness. We see the threads that connect together all of life; we see how each part reflects the whole.

> Whoever can't see the whole in every part plays
>   at blind man's bluff;
> A wise man tastes the Tigris in every sip.[12]

CONNECTIONS OF LIGHT

In our deeper knowing we understand this deep connectedness of all of life. And yet the church, the rise of Western science, and a growing culture of materialism have effectively banished the *anima mundi* from our collective imagination, until, in the words of Jung, "man himself has ceased to be the microcosm and his anima is no longer the consubstantial *scintilla* or spark of the *anima mundi*, the World Soul."[13] How can we redeem this relationship, recreate this connection in our imagination and inner work? How can we return our light to the World Soul?

Once we make the simple acknowledgment that we are a part of the whole, then a connection is made between our light and the world. We make this connection with our consciousness and with our imagination; then through this connection our light begins to flow. In this way we begin to redeem the work of the whole. These connections create pathways of light that find their way through the darkness of the collective psyche. Just as in our personal psyche, there are blocks and places of resistance to this flow of light; and there are also places of power, creativity, and unexpected qualities.

The World Soul is not a fixed or defined substance, but a living substance made out of the hopes, dreams, and deepest imaginings of humanity and of all creation. This is the home of creation's collective memories and the myths of humanity. Here are the archetypes and powers that define our life. Here are hidden places of magical meaning, places where dreams can come into being. We have lived for so long in the stark barrenness of a rational landscape that we have forgotten the potency that lies beneath the surface. Flowing through the pathways created by our conscious connection to the *anima mundi*, our light will find its way to places of power that are within the world, places where deeper layers of meaning are waiting to come alive.

We presently see the material world as something apart from ourselves, a solid and enduring object without life or magic. Like the seventeenth-century scientists who decided animals had no feelings and thus could be dissected without suffering, we feel free to inflict our will upon our world, pillaging it for our own gain without any thought to the suffering and damage we are subjecting it to. Caught up in our materialistic drives, we may not recognize that this image of the world is an illusion, an insubstantial dream that can easily alter or dissolve as new forces come into play. As our light makes its connections within the World Soul, it will activate some of these forces, energies that are waiting to liberate the world from this destructive illusion. We know how this works in our own alchemical journey, how what we find beneath the surface changes our values in unexpected ways, how connections are then made and synchronicities occur that before would have been unbelievable. As we make these connections, we will begin to see that the world and our own selves both are more magical than we know.

This work of connecting our light to the world does not need to be done through a mass movement, or by millions of people. For centuries a few alchemists held these secrets of inner transformation against the powerful forces of the church and the establishment. The real work is always done by a small number of individuals. What matters is the level of participation: whether we dare to make a real commitment to the work of the soul. Unlike the alchemists living in their laboratories, we do not need to give up our ordinary outer life—everyday life can also be a necessary balance and protection against the strange delusions so easily created by the inner world. But we do need to recognize that there is a certain work that needs to be done, and that we can no longer stand on the sidelines and watch our collective dreams spin out of control.

Our culture may have isolated us within our individual self, separated us from the magic of life—but once again this is just a surface mirage. We are all connected and part of the living substance of creation. Within every cell of our being, every spark of consciousness, we have a knowing of oneness. Our own inner journey cannot be separate from the journey of the whole. An inner journey separate from the whole is no real journey; it is just another illusion created by an ego that wants to protect itself.

The substance of our soul is part of the fabric of life, the tapestry of creation in which are woven the unicorns and monsters of our dreams as well as the skyscrapers of our cities. The inner and outer worlds are not separate—despite all the efforts of our rational culture to have us believe they are. The recent dramas of terrorism have once again brought demons into our living rooms, and we sense there is nowhere really safe from these shadows. But we do not need to simply be victims of these archetypal nightmares. By evoking the real magic that comes from within, we can work to balance the light and the dark, and creatively participate in changing the dreams that define our collective life.

The light of the World Soul is waiting to be used to connect us with the inner powers that belong to matter and to life itself. The real world is an enchanted place, full of magical powers waiting to be used. And, as the alchemists understood, the *anima mundi* is a creative force: "it is the artist, the craftsperson, the 'inner Vision' which shapes and differentiates the prime matter, giving it form."[14]

AWAKENING TO THE PURPOSE OF CREATION

The World Soul is not just a psychological or philosophical concept. It is a living spiritual substance within us and around us. Just as the individual soul pervades the whole human being—our body, thoughts, and feelings—the nature of the World Soul is that it is present within everything. It pervades all of creation, and is a unifying principle within the world. The alchemist-physician Thomas Browne saw it as "the Universal Spirit of Nature, the *anima mundi* or World Soul responsible for all phenomena and which binds all life together."[15] Marsilio Ficino saw the World Soul flourishing everywhere:

> The soul is all things together....And since it is the center of all things, it has the forces of all. Hence it passes into all things. And since it is the true connection of all things, it goes to the one without leaving the others....therefore it may rightly be called the center of nature, the middle term of all things, the face of all, the bond and juncture of the universe."[16]

The Soul of the World permeates all of creation like salt in water. The physical world is the denser plane, and within it and sustaining it is the reality of the soul, which contains the Higher Intelligence that is the creative and ordering principle of life.

This divine intelligence is in everything. It is the spark within matter, the light within a human being. When we isolate ourself from our own soul, we deny ourself conscious access to this light, to its guidance and intelligence. Then our life becomes without meaning or purpose, "a walking shadow...signifying nothing." Without real purpose, our life is just a physical existence. When we reconnect with our soul, the magic and meaning of life come alive both within us and around us.

Our real gift to life is an awareness of its purpose. When we are aware of life's purpose, the light of the soul shines in our life, and its secret hidden within the world comes alive. And the light that is within us is within everything; it is "at the center of all things." When our light comes alive within us, it comes alive within all of creation. It reveals to creation its true purpose. At the present time our collective culture sees life primarily from a material perspective—we worship the god of consumerism, making acquisition our life's goal. We are imprisoned within matter. We have forgotten the symbolic and sacred meaning of the outer world. Alien-ated from our soul, we have alienated creation from its deeper meaning. And because we have denied the world its divinity, it is slowly dying.

The real alchemical work is to liberate creation from this imprisonment—to awaken life to its meaning. We have to free the light that is within us and within the world. A transcendent image of the divine will only give us access to a transcendent light. We need the light hidden in matter, the gold that is within lead. When this light comes alive within life, it can change the patterns of creation and create the forms of the future that will bring life back into harmony. It can manifest its unify-ing nature.

The alchemists understood the nature of this light:

It is the father of every miraculous work in the
    whole world....
Its power is perfect if it is converted to earth.[17]

Working within the world, this power *is* the light and power of the divine made manifest. The light that is within our own psyche *is* the light within the *anima mundi*. In the depth of ourself we discover this essential oneness. This is the same awareness as the yogi's realization that one's true nature and unchanging self (*atman*) is the Universal Self (*Atman*). What is within us is within everything. Once we understand this truth, we step outside of the parameters of our individual self and come to realize the power that is within us. This shift in awareness is a very simple step that has profound consequences.

IMAGINING THE WORLD

At the moment, the world is asleep, suffering the dreams of humanity, which have become a nightmare of desecration and pollution. In our hubris we have forgotten that the world is more than our collective projections, that it is more mysterious and strange than our rational minds would like us to believe. Quantum physics has revealed a fluid and unpredictable world, in which consciousness and matter are not separate—whether a photon of light behaves as a particle or wave depends upon the consciousness of the observer. But we remain within the images of Newtonian physics: matter that is dead, definable, and solid, and consciousness that is objective, safely divorced from the physical world. Matter and spirit remain split, and we continue in the patriarchal fantasy that we can have control over our world.

As we have already seen, the physical world was not always experienced as so isolated. Many cultures have been more concerned with the relationship between the worlds. In the medieval imagination the physical world was just one part of the Great Chain of Being. Medieval cathedrals imaged a symbolic and geometric relationship between the different parts, with the maze that symbolized our journey through this world mirroring the rose window's image of a higher reality of light. In the Sufism of Ibn 'Arabî, the worlds were seen as connected by the symbolic world of the imagination, which acts as a bridge or an "intermediary between the world of Mystery (*'âlâm al-ghayb*) and the world of Visibility (*'âlâm al-shahâdat*)."

In their retorts and crucibles the alchemists were working not just with chemical substances but also with the inner energies of life. Their symbolic writings describe both the mixture of tinctures and the marriage of the king and queen, the union of sun and moon. The alchemists took their work seriously, knowing the real responsibility involved.[18] They knew that they were working with a secret substance in life, "mercury" or "quicksilver," a catalyst that can transform whatever it touches. The way their chemicals changed and transformed imaged how life can be changed with the correct mixture of ingredients. They knew that matter and spirit are not separate. Modern science is now revealing the same thing to us. Yet how the inner and outer worlds relate, and how our consciousness affects the physical world, remain for us still a great mystery.

Once we surrender our safe concept of a separate, static, and defined world, we open to a more dynamic reality in which life is an energy field with which our consciousness and unconscious interact: a pulsating Indra's Net being continually woven by the soul, through which our consciousness takes on form, our dreams come into being.

LIBERATING THE ANIMA MUNDI

We need the magical powers within nature in order to heal and transform our world. But awakening these powers would mean that our patriarchal institutions will lose their control, as once again the mysterious inner world will come into play, releasing forces once understood and used by the priestess and shaman, whose existence the patriarchal world has forgotten. The science of the future will work with these forces, exploring how the different worlds interrelate, including how the energies of the inner can be used in the outer. The shaman and the scientist will work together, the wisdom of the priestess and the wisdom of the physician renew their ancient connection.

But the first step is to awaken these powers, not just individually but for the whole world. We are moving into a global era, and any real changes need to be made globally. If we try to grasp powers for our own individual use, we risk descending into black magic, which is the use of inner powers for the purposes of the ego. Our next step in evolution is to realize the primal truth of oneness and to reunite our individual light with the whole.

The work pioneered by Jung has given us access to the science of alchemy, revealing this hidden part of our Western esoteric tradition. Psychological techniques have been developed to help reveal an inner world of energy, power, and creative potential. We no longer need to stay locked in the surface world. But our tendency has been to take this access for our individual selves, our own inner journey, and not realize its larger implications.

Real alchemical work was always for the sake of the whole. In our inner journey, our own alchemical process, to work for the sake of the whole means to acknowledge the dimension of the *anima mundi*. The light we discover in our own depths is a spark of the World Soul, and the world needs this light in order to evolve. When we make this connection in our consciousness and our imagination, we begin to change the fabric of life. The alchemists knew the potency of this spark, this philosophical mercury. The same substance that transforms our individual self is the primordial world-creating spirit, the "universal and scintillating fire in the light of nature, which carries the heavenly spirit with it." When we liberate it within ourselves but do not claim it just for ourselves, solely for our own inner process, we create certain connections through which this energy can flow into the core of life. We participate in the alchemical work of liberating the *anima mundi*. This is the first step in the work.

What does it really mean, to liberate the *anima mundi*? In our individual alchemical *opus* we experience the effects of freeing the light, energy, and creative potential that lie within us. We know how this liberation can radically change our vision and experience of life. We are taken into a different dimension of our self, and life begins to magically open doors that before were closed or hidden. Of course these changes are not always what we may want—they do not fulfill our surface desires, but they have a deeper meaning and purpose. Something within us awakens and the life of the spirit begins. The alchemists understood that the individual is a microcosm of the whole, and that what can happen to each of us can happen to the world.

When the light of the soul returns, a grey world of drudgery begins to sparkle; the multihued qualities of creation become visible. Instead of the endless pursuit of pleasure, life beckons us on a search for meaning: the colors of life speak to us, telling us their story, singing to us their song. The music of life returns, a music that *is* creation alive. A real dialogue between our inner self and our outer life begins to unfold as we directly participate in the hidden mystery of life coming alive: it comes alive within ourself and within the world. In the light of the soul the barriers between inner and outer dissolve, and we no longer have to dig beneath the surface for some semblance of purpose to our lives.

The light of the soul returning to the *anima mundi* will free us from the stranglehold of materialism, because it will awaken us to different qualities within life, give us different dreams to follow. In this light we will see life differently; a different world will become visible. When matter is dead and the soul is asleep, we are easily seduced by the attractions of materialism: we see nothing else to fulfill us. But we know in our own journey how we can suddenly be awakened to a different reality that was always around us and yet hidden from sight, a world that does not belong to buying and selling but to the mystery of the soul. Then a sense of wonder and awe returns. The same can happen with the world. We are longing to participate in a life that is multidimensional and full of beauty rather than just pursuing our own pleasure. Who would not turn from lust to love? The light of the soul is the spirit within matter that makes life dance. It awakens us to the simple joy of what is:

> i thank You God for most this amazing
> day:for the leaping greenly spirits of trees
> and a blue true dream of sky;and for everything
> which is natural which is infinite which is yes
>
> (i who have died am alive again today,
> and this is the sun's birthday;this is the birth
> day of life and of love and wings:and of the gay
> great happening illimitably earth)[19]

This is the world into which we were born. Even our city streets and shopping malls are alive in a way that is presently veiled. Creation is sparkling in so many ways, though its spectrum of colors is at present only partly visible. We have created a prison of materialism, but it is just an illusion. If we let life speak to us, it will show us the way to unlock this door, pull down these walls, dissolve this nightmare. There are forces within life more powerful than our corporations and politicians. And these forces do not play by the rules we have created. With laughter and a glint of mischief, they can rearrange our lives.

Our world is presently asleep. Its magical powers are for the most part dormant, but they are present, waiting to be used to transform our world. We have confined miracles to the safety of small events, but the whole world is miraculous. We may talk about the "miracle of life," but we place this miracle within the safe container of what we expect to happen. We do not dare to recognize that a real miracle is the unexpected, the divine waking up in life. We may try to block off this dimension that is pure joy and light, to remain within the confines of our egos and expectations. But to do that is to deny the divinity of creation, deny that there is an Intelligence continually recreating the world according to divine principles that are beyond our rational understanding.

On our individual inner journey we begin to glimpse the workings of our soul, how it helps to create our outer life in an often miraculous way, as well as rearranging our inner selves. As we turn away from the ego towards the soul, we see more of its power and purpose. Its light is the ordering principle in our lives; it can create harmony out of the disparate aspects of our psyche, bring the mandala of the Self into being. Through the workings of the soul we begin to have an outer life in balance with our inner self. It is no different for the world. The *anima mundi* is the ordering and creative principle in creation. Without her presence we experience only the fractious elements of our egos, the greed, insecurity, and power dynamics that are so visible in our contemporary landscape. When her light is awakened, then she can bring the world into harmony and balance. This simple and radical truth was known to the alchemists: it is the light hidden in matter that will redeem the world.

THE LIGHT OF
THE HEART

*The Sun of Light has risen in the heart.
It shines and there is no setting.*

al-Hakîm at-Tirmidhî[1]

SPIRITUAL KNOWLEDGE OF THE HEART

We have within us the consciousness and power that we need for individual and global transformation. The center of this transformative consciousness is in the heart. If we are to live our mystical potential and participate fully at this time of transition, we need to understand the mystical science of the heart. Then we can learn to use this spiritual organ as a means for global healing and awakening.

The human heart is a multidimensional organ of spiritual awareness and light. And as the human being is a microcosm of the whole of creation, the world itself has a heart of spiritual awareness and light. At its core, the human heart is one with the heart of the world, making the individual a doorway to the love and divine mystery of the whole. As we enter the chambers of our own heart, we can access and work with the divine consciousness of the world.

The mysteries of love, the science of the heart, have been revealed throughout the centuries in the esoteric knowledge of various mystical traditions. In particular, Sufism has made an extensive study of the human heart and its spiritual nature, expanding on how the spiritual organs within the heart transform and awaken the wayfarer, leading to a more complete spiritual awareness, a deepening immersion in the divine light of unification. Sufi wayfarers have mapped the journey into the inner worlds, showing how the awakening of the heart's spiritual centers expands the seeker's consciousness. They describe how, ultimately, in the heart's innermost chamber—the heart of hearts—the lover finally merges with the divine, completing the mystical journey from separation to union.

Much of this knowledge of the spiritual organ of the heart focuses on the interior journey of the wayfarer. However, there is another dimension of the science of the heart that until now has been kept hidden. This is how the heart of the individual can interact spiritually with the whole of life. As we enter a new era in consciousness, these mysteries will become part of our greater understanding, and we will be given specific knowledge of how the individual relates to the whole, and how the inner relates to the outer. Within the heart, all the different levels of reality are connected together; the inner flows directly into the outer.

Critical to this new dimension of our awareness is the recognition of how the human being is a microcosm of the whole. As we begin to understand this relationship, our sense of spiritual life and how we can be of service will change. So too will our understanding of how ordinary life and spiritual life interrelate, and how the inner world can nourish the outer. But to take this step in awareness, we must begin by shifting our focus away from our own personal journey, allowing a greater unfolding to reveal itself.

THE INDIVIDUAL AS MICROCOSM

This knowledge of the coming era reflects how the individual functions as a microcosm of the whole and how the heart works as the direct spiritual connection between the individual and the whole. Man's pivotal position as a microcosm of creation can be found in Western spirituality in the tradition of alchemy. For the alchemists, man is "an image of the great world, and is called the microcosm or little world."[2]

In Sufism every human being is "made in the image of God." Ibn 'Arabî describes how the *hadith* "God created Adam upon His own form" holds both for the great Adam, who is the cosmos in its entirety, and for the small Adam, who is the human being, and who is the microcosm. He explains:

> "He placed within man every one of His attributes, just as He placed all of His attributes within the cosmos." And the three basic worlds of the macrocosm—the spiritual, imaginal, and corporeal—are represented in man by the spirit (*rûh*), soul (*nafs*), and body (*jism*).[3]

Part of the esoteric significance of the relationship of macrocosm and microcosm is how the spiritual centers within the individual correspond to the whole of creation, its spiritual as well as physical body. Thus, in order to explore the relationship of microcosm and macrocosm, we need to recognize that the planet as a whole is a living spiritual body, also made in the image of God. Then we can understand the relationship of microcosm and macrocosm as belonging not only to the exterior physical world, but to all of the spiritual worlds, all of the interior dimensions; and we can see how an individual's spiritual centers, in particular the heart and its chambers, are central to this relationship.

The heart is a doorway between different levels of reality, existing in the physical world as well as in the realm of pure being and Absolute Truth. The heart of an awakened human being has direct access to the heart of the world. If we think of ourself as separate from the whole of creation, we are not able to claim this connection, this inner affinity. But when we recognize the oneness of which we are all a part, then this connection comes alive and the heart can function as a dynamic spiritual center in which different levels of reality are aligned together.

This alignment enables the individual to directly affect the whole in the same way that the heart affects the whole human being. When we feel His love within the heart, the whole body rejoices. Nothing is excluded as the whole human being is directly nourished by the pure substance of divine love. As we come to understand the correspondence between the heart of the individual and the heart of the world, we will begin to unveil the mysteries of how the awakened mystic can directly affect the whole of life, and how this connection of the heart can be used to benefit life.

CHAMBERS OF THE HEART

The heart is the spiritual center of the human being. It is the home of the Self, our divine nature. "That Person in the heart, no bigger than a thumb, is known as maker of past and future....That is Self."[4]

As the home of the Self, the heart is where our spiritual life unfolds, where we open to the inner reality of life and perceive the real meaning of the outer world. It is also in the heart that the microcosm and macrocosm meet. Through the heart we can perceive the infinite nature of our real Self, which is both individual and universal. The Self *is* the whole and thus within the heart we have direct access to the whole.

The heart is also where the energy structure of the planet and the energy structure, or spiritual body, of the individual directly meet. It is through the heart that we can work most efficiently with the spiritual body of the planet, just as through the heart we can work most efficiently with our own spiritual body.

How do we work with the heart for the sake of the whole? How can we use the heart as a way of helping the spiritual evolution of the planet? For the Sufi the simplest answer is love. Unconditional love takes us into the heart where it activates our spiritual Self, transforming us and the world around us.

As some schools of Sufism have explored, there are different chambers or spiritual centers within the heart, each center corresponding to different dimensions of the inner world and to different levels of spiritual consciousness.

As early as the ninth century, al-Hakîm at-Tirmidhî wrote *A Treatise on the Heart,* in which he differentiated between four chambers of the heart: the breast (*sadr*), the heart (*qalb*), the inner heart (*fu'âd*), and the intellect (*lubb*). At-Tirmidhî describes the different qualities of spiritual awareness—the different lights—which belong to each chamber, with the innermost chamber having "the light of unification and the light of the contemplation of the uniqueness of God."[5]

Over the centuries Sufi teaching developed its study of the esoteric nature of the spiritual heart and explored how the heart functions within the spiritual development of the individual. In the ninth century Junayd cultivated the concept of the *latâ'if*, or subtle spiritual centers or organs of knowledge within the heart.[6] Later Sufi masters developed an understanding of the *latâ'if* as seven or ten subtle centers or receptors of divine energy that comes from more subtle cosmic realms.[7] Part of the spiritual science of the *latâ'if* is that these different spiritual centers within the heart correspond to different dimensions of the inner world; by activating a specific center, or *latîfah*, the wayfarer can travel in the corresponding interior realm.

Sufi masters developed practices and meditations to work with the energy of the heart, using different *dhikrs* and meditations for the different *latâ'if*. Traditionally the practitioner would progress gradually from one level to another over the course of his spiritual life. Each *latîfah* would open him to a different level of reality, and to the light and spiritual energy that belong to that level.

Part of the development of each level is learning to work with its energy so that it flows throughout the human being, bringing light and love where they are needed, helping the wayfarer to evolve. Finally, at the level of unification, all distinctions between lover and Beloved dissolve, and there is only His light shining through the human being. This is the complete realization that we are "made in the image of God." All is He.

A NEW PERSPECTIVE ON THE PATH

Through the eyes of the individual, the wayfarer journeys deeper and deeper into love, into the heart, through different stages that mark his spiritual progress. And yet we know that this is only a limited perspective, because the real nature of the path is not a journey with stages, but the continual unfolding of love that happens moment by moment in and out of time. The great ninth-century mystic Bâyezîd Bistâmî came to realize this wider view:

> At the beginning I was mistaken in four respects. I concerned myself to remember God, to know Him, to love Him and to seek Him. When I had come to the end I saw that He had remembered me before I remembered Him, that His knowledge of me had preceded my knowledge of Him, that His love towards me had existed before my love to Him and He had sought me before I sought Him.

When we recognize the divine at the center of spiritual life, a very different picture emerges: there is no "journey" because the realization is that it is not about us—it is not about the wayfarer but about a continual revelation of His love. His love is always complete and yet it is continually being revealed in the hearts of those who love Him.

The danger is always when we define spiritual life by the image we have created. Often at the end of "the journey" the wayfarer realizes the truth that there is no journey because there is nowhere to go. The divine is not other than us—this is the truth reflected in the parable of the fishes who search for water. Then all concepts of spiritual life fall away and instead there is a deepening immersion in His oneness and also in the emptiness that underlies creation.

Often the mystic is confronted by the difficulties of "bringing back" an understanding of this reality, which is why many lovers prefer silence. However, in the Naqshbandi teachings on the *latâ'if*, after the experience of the most hidden (*akhfâ*), the divine light of Truth, the wayfarer returns to the *latîfah* of the *nafs*, the lower self, and the other *latâ'if* related to the world of creation (air [*bâd*], fire [*nâr*], water [*mâ*], and earth [*khâk*]). The Naqshbandi have always stressed the importance of returning to the world of forms after being immersed in the formless.

The ability of the mystic to go beyond form and then return to the relative world allows her to live in a way that is dynamically alive to the moment, rather than caught in an image that belongs to the past. Unidentified with form, the mystic keeps open the gates of revelation, knowing that, in the words of Abû Tâlib al-Makkî, "God never discloses Himself in a single form to two individuals or in the same form twice."[8] Part of the contribution of the mystic, one who has journeyed into the formless, is to remind humanity of the divine's indefinable nature, to keep a place of remembrance that does not crystallize Him in any form or name.

In an era concerned with the development of the individual, and in particular the development of individual consciousness, the images of the path reflected this perspective: the individual wayfarer journeys towards an expanded spiritual consciousness. But we are moving into a new era in which our physical sciences, like particle physics and ecology, are giving us images of a dynamic, interdependent reality in which our sense of separation is an illusion. What matters now is the unifying principle of oneness and how the individual can contribute to the whole. In this field, spiritual science can contribute its knowledge of the interrelated dynamics of oneness and how energy works in the inner worlds. The heart, as an organ of direct perception and awareness of oneness, has a central role to play in this developing consciousness.

NOURISHING THE WORLD

There is a mystical science of how the heart of an awakened individual can be aligned with the energy structure of the planet and be used to awaken and nourish life. While the mystical journey appears to be a turning away from the world, it actually embraces life in its innermost essence. From this central position the mystic can most directly help life change and evolve. The mystic has always played this role, but for millennia it has been veiled, hidden even from the spiritual practitioner.

The heart is at the center of the human being and therefore at the center of life. Because the heart is a microcosm of the whole, it can speak directly to the Soul of the World. It can help clear the debris that is covering the world, and help the world be cleansed by love so that it shines more brightly and radiantly. An awakened heart can be used to help free life from negative patterns and attitudes.

Central to this science is that the heart naturally functions within the plane of unity, the dimension of the Self. In this dimension of oneness, to which the heart gives us access, everything is present in each moment and there are no constrictions of time and space. This means that within the heart we are free to be where we are needed. Love can flow directly from the Source—our inner light can go directly where it can be of service to life in the inner and outer worlds, not hindered by the darkness of the physical world. This potential is reflected in spiritual practices of global healing in which one places the entire world within one's heart and nourishes it with one's light and love. If needed, one can then consciously direct one's attention and love to places of darkness or suffering.

Once we acknowledge the relationship of macrocosm and microcosm within the oneness of life, it becomes apparent how our forgetfulness, our attitudes and actions have caused pain to the Soul of the World. We have damaged the inner structures of light and love that nourish our planet; we have created dark clouds in the inner worlds that obscure us from the light. Our values are having a global effect, not only to our physical ecosystem but to the spiritual body of the planet.

We are only beginning to take responsibility for the effects of our actions in the outer, physical world, but many people feel the damage that has been caused in the inner, feeling a loss of faith, a loss of joy and hope, and not knowing its cause. The Soul of the World is crying out to be saved. It is the responsibility of spiritually awake human beings to respond to this cry—to allow our hearts to be used for this work.

We know how central love is to our own life, how it nourishes us in our very depths. A mother's love for her child is something fundamental to life. Through the light and warmth of love we grow and expand and are able to realize our true potential as human beings. Love helps us to evolve through all the stages of life, from childhood to partnerships and parenthood.

One of the wonders of the path is how we can be loved directly from the Source, experiencing His love within the heart. This is a love that is not caught in any pattern of relationship or the dynamics of projection. It is pure love that flows into the heart from the inner planes. It comes through the chambers of the heart, directly connecting lover and Beloved, nourishing us in ways beyond our imaginings. It opens us to the reality of His presence and awakens us to the real purpose of our life. It also transforms us, activating spiritual energy centers and our higher centers of consciousness.

What is true for the individual is true for the whole of creation. "In the whole of the universe there are only Two: the Lover and the Beloved. God loves His Creation, and the Soul loves God."[9] Through the heart He can nourish all levels of life. Sometimes we experience this directly, as a sweetness or energy of love flows through our heart to a person we are with. But love flows through an awakened heart to all of creation, to the trees and the grass and even inanimate objects—because everything is hungry for love. The whole of the world is a lover waiting for the Beloved.

Love comes into the physical world, spinning the atoms of creation with the remembrance of God. Love also comes from the Source into the inner realms, into the archetypal world of life's primal energies, and into the world of the soul.[10] The archetypes, the gods of the ancient world, need our love and attention, as some schools of psychology are now recognizing. These primordial forces that are the foundation of life respond to love, sometimes turning from resentful, angry beings into helpful and supportive forces, as is imaged in many fairy tales and tribal stories.

Love can free the archetypes of negative patterns and blocks that restrict the beneficial flow of their energy. Shamans traditionally work primarily in the archetypal world, and know the importance of relating to these forces with attention, respect, and love. Because love is such a powerful transformative force, it can directly affect these inner energies, enabling them to awaken to a higher and more creative potential.

For many years I worked in the inner world directly with the archetypes and witnessed the changes that love and attention can bring. I saw how empty barren inner landscapes could be planted with seeds of hope, which were tended with love, and how the landscape then became an orchard with fruit that nourished the soul and brought joy to life. I met a woman whose tears had blinded her eyes, so she could not see or look after her children. Through love she began to see and heal, and her children were no longer abandoned. Love brought healing and magic to the inner world, and the song of the future became alive. The child with stars in her eyes came to greet me, and showed me the dawn that was waiting for humanity. I saw a new prayer being given, which was also a seed opening to the sun. Love can heal the inner world that has been abused by centuries of rationalism and forgetfulness.

Love can also directly heal the soul. Through love we can speak to the soul of another person, not just to the ego or personality. There are ancient ways to welcome the soul of a newborn child into the world, rituals of the heart that allow the infant not to forget her true nature so that the bond between soul and ego is not clouded or severed by life, but nourishes the person throughout life.

And the heart can speak to the soul of an adult, healing wounds that the ego's or our culture's forgetfulness have inflicted. Some souls have been wounded by events in their life, by tragedy, heartbreak, or acts that caused suffering to others. Through the heart, light can be given to lift the dark clouds that surround such a soul, a darkness that is often experienced as depression. Because meaning comes from the inner, when our soul is veiled by such darkness life can become meaningless: we have lost the light of the soul. Love can restore it.

THE WORK OF THE LOVER

Working with love means that we respond from the core of our being to our global predicament. We can no longer afford to be isolated within our own spiritual practices or individual lives. We need to make an inner commitment to the spiritual life of the whole. We need to recognize the need and thus enable our Higher Self to respond.

There is a Sufi saying, "It is the consent which draws down the grace." When we say "yes," we allow ourself to be used. Without our willing participation, the gates of grace remain closed. This is one of the secrets of free will.

How does the heart know where to respond? The wonder of the heart is that because it contains our higher spiritual intelligence, it instinctively knows where its attention and love are needed. The heart opens in response to a call. And the heart can differentiate a true need, just as a mother knows when the cry of her child is a cry of real pain or just a demand for attention.

Through the different chambers of the heart, love works on different levels, from the outer to the innermost where the Truth is hidden. Through these different vehicles of love, the lover can bring love where it is needed, helping to heal a wounded world and also to activate energy centers that are dormant within the world. The lover has tasted the transformative nature of His love, and knows its potential. *What can be given to the individual can be given to the world.* This is one of the secrets of global unity, of the emerging state of global awareness.

In our individual prayers, meditation, and devotions we work to be inwardly attentive and to align ourself with the Source. Awareness of the breath is one way to align with the Source, as we attune ourself to the basic rhythm of life, our awareness flowing on the out-breath from the inner world of the soul into manifestation and on the in-breath returning to the Source. A *dhikr* or *mantra* is another practice of inner alignment, as our consciousness is attuned to a divine name and That which it names. Another practice, already mentioned, begins a meditation or prayer by placing the world within the heart, reminding one of the all-inclusive nature of one's practice.

The heart of the disciple can also be used and directed by her teacher, by one to whom she has surrendered in love. This is one of the secrets of spiritual transmission, the transmission of love from master to disciple. When the teacher awakens the disciple's heart with the transmission of love, there is a bond of love created between the disciple and the teacher and the whole of the spiritual lineage. Through this bond of love the disciple is given the love and light that are needed to help her along the path. Because this bond belongs to the inner plane of the soul, physical presence is often not needed for the transmission of love. Through this bond the teacher can also direct the heart of the disciple for the work in the world, transmit love and light through her heart directly to where it is needed.

The love that comes through this chain of transmission is often at a higher frequency than the disciple can access on her own. Because the love is on a higher frequency than the personal self, it can flow through the heart without any interference. Thus energy can be given through the disciple that is needed for the work in the world rather than the individual's spiritual development.

The energy needed by the world is not always the same as that designed to help the individual. It is important to realize that there may be a distinction between spiritual energy needed for the planet and that needed for individual spiritual life. For example, at the present time there is a dense and very powerful energy needed by the planet that is very impersonal, cold, and hard and cannot function on the level of individual development. It has a very specific purpose, which is to realign the whole planet with its Source, and also to awaken certain energy centers within the planet.[11] An individual or a spiritual group surrendered in love, under the protection and guidance of a spiritual master, can transmit this energy.

SPIRITUAL GROUPS

A spiritual group can be a powerful and beneficial organism of light and love in the world. Spiritual energy can be transmitted to the world through a group, or a spiritual tradition. A group that meets regularly for spiritual practice has a group heart that sustains the group and also functions as a vehicle for spiritual energy. The efficiency of this spiritual organ depends upon the sincerity of the group, the level of development of its participants, and whether they are under the protection and guidance of a spiritual teacher. These factors also determine the level of energy to which they have access. The members of a group help each other on their individual journeys, but, bonded by their devotion and a shared spiritual purpose, they can also be used for the work of the whole.

Every group has a different vibration, which determines the level of its participation and where it has access in the outer and inner worlds. Some spiritual groups work in the outer worlds, helping with healing or to improve the outer conditions of people's lives. Other groups work close to the physical world, helping to heal the etheric body of the earth, while other groups may work in the archetypal or angelic worlds, and still others work deep in the inner, even in the planes of non-being.

Spiritual groups form part of the spiritual body of the earth, its body of light. Seen from this perspective, the groups are not separate, independent entities, but part of an organic, living being. They are formed where they are needed by the spiritual body of the earth, where their love and light need to constellate. Throughout the history of the earth, spiritual energy and activity have focused in different physical locations. In more recent centuries India and Tibet have been the locality of much spiritual work, while the flowering of Sufism in the earlier part of the millennium points to a spiritual focus in the Middle East, although Genghis Khan and his Mogul warriors brought devastation to much of that region, causing many Sufis to migrate west to Damascus and Anatolia. In recent years many different traditions have moved from the East to the West, which appears to be the present focus of much spiritual energy and activity.

As a living, spiritual being, the earth changes, its focus of light moves, and the spiritual work that is done by practitioners changes. Our focus on the individual dimension of spiritual work often overlooks this larger, global picture; it misses the way spiritual groups and their work are all interrelated. Sadly, many present-day practitioners remain isolated within the image of their own path as something separate rather than embracing a vision of dynamic wholeness in which each practitioner is like a different cell in the light body of the planet, not recognizing how the different spiritual paths and traditions are just different ways of working with the one light.

It is only when we are working together that we can overcome many of the present obstacles created by global consumerism and the desecration it inflicts on the planet. When the different paths are linked together in the inner and outer worlds, they will realize their real transformative potential and help the world awaken.

Much spiritual work is veiled, hidden in the inner worlds. But sometimes we are given a glimpse of the nature of this work. A friend had the following vision, which images some of the work of the Naqshbandi order, guided by the presence of its founder, the thirteenth-century master Abd al-Khalîq al-Ghujduwânî:

> During the meditation I found myself, after a short journey of the soul away from the earth, in a gigantic space station outside of our galaxy in the universe. Suddenly I found myself in a control room standing to the right of Sheikh Ghujduwânî. Around us there were only shining and blinking computers and control panels.
>
> Through the windows I could see, below us to the right, our galaxy, with the beautiful earth against a black background. I also saw energy- and light-canals which reached to other galaxies.
>
> Sheikh Ghujduwânî explained much to me about his current work. Some of it I could hold on to.
>
> He said he now creates connections on various levels of reality to other living galaxies so that there can be a connection between them and ours. Various dark powers endlessly try to hinder

this. However, they do not succeed, since divine evolution and the power of love and surrender of the masters are stronger. Saying this, he laughed deeply and cheerily.

Then I looked to our beautiful brightly shining planet, which was enclosed in gray and black zones like fog. Through the fog an energy spiral spun very fast, on various levels of existence. At the same time I recognized this spiral as the energy field of our order. This spiral, fed through the love and surrender of meditators, slowly dissolves this fog of divine forgetting and of darkness on various levels of existence.

The Sheikh said he was working at this place in the universe in order to balance out certain energies between the galaxies, and to protect these galaxies, including our own. He works always under order from the Almighty.

He doesn't work alone; he works also with Buddhist teachers and masters.

This vision takes the friend away from the earth to where a vaster dimension of spiritual work is revealed, work that is creating "connections on various levels of reality to other living galaxies." Just as connections and patterns of relationship are being created in our world as different groups and spiritual traditions are being linked together, other connections and relationships are being formed in the vaster macrocosm. Then the vision shows the work of the Naqshbandi Sufi order in this world, creating an energy field that dissolves the fog of forgetfulness and darkness that covers our planet. This energy field, "fed through the love and surrender of meditators," is "on various levels of existence," because the fog of forgetfulness and the darkness that need to be dissolved also exist on different levels. Our culture has created pollution and darkness far into the inner worlds. An important aspect of real spiritual work is its ability to function on different levels, to work in the hidden, inner worlds. The different centers within the heart, the *latâ'if*, give us access to different levels of reality, and through the guidance of our superiors we work together to bring the energy of the path where it is needed.

In its final statement, the vision shows that the different paths are not working in isolation: "He doesn't work alone; he works also with Buddhist teachers and masters." The coming era is one of cooperation and interrelationship. Within the heart everything is one. Just as the heart can reconnect an individual with the unity inherent within him, so can it connect us with the unity of all life. When we bring this consciousness into life, we recognize that we are all working together for the sake of the whole.

THE AXIS OF LOVE

*Love is the principle of existence
and its cause;
it is the beginning of the world
and what maintains it.*

Ibn 'Arabî[1]

THE WORLD SPINS ON AN AXIS OF LOVE

The axis of love runs through creation, carrying the
energy of love to every atom. The axis of love brings color
to the world, all the different hues and variations of His
love that give meaning and beauty to life. Without it
there would be no joy, no hope, no love present in the
world.

The axis of love sings the song of His creation, the
joy of His manifestation, the real wonder of His world.
It is the axis of "He loves them and they love Him," in
which all of life is a lover longing for the Beloved. This
gravitational pull of His love holds life together; it gives
meaning and sustenance to all of creation.

The axis of love spins at a very high frequency, which
makes it almost invisible even to the inner eye, but it is
a very powerful core of energy that nourishes life more
than we realize. Like the magnetic core of the earth, the

axis of love creates a magnetic field that protects our planet from forces of darkness. It also speaks to the heart of every seeker who turns towards God, reminding us of our true nature and of the love that is in the core of our being. In a more diffuse way it nourishes all of creation, reminding each atom of its Creator and of the bond of love between the Creator and His creation.

It is part of the wonder of the way the world is created that this axis of love is present in every grain of sand, every drop of rain, every laugh, every tear. But the density of the world limits the flow of His love through it. Human darkness, greed, and corruption add to the density, creating negative energy fields that can be clearly seen on the inner planes. Thus the natural flow of love and light that should nourish life in the inner and outer worlds has become blocked. The spread of material values that deny the sacredness of the earth has made this problem global. There are very few places left where the energy can flow freely, just as there are few places in the physical world that remain unpolluted. The collective attitude of humanity has a powerful effect on the inner nourishment of the world.

Because the heart of the mystic belongs to her Beloved, she can bypass many of the patterns of resistance that block the flow of love and light around the world. The axis of love is most directly accessible through the heart, because the heart is our organ of divine perception and divine love. Through the heart we are aligned with the center of our being and with the axis of love that runs through creation. Through those who love Him, whose hearts He has awakened, His love flows into the world and the axis of love is consciously present—it is not veiled as in the hearts of those who follow their own desires, who know only the dimension of their own ego-self. His lovers carry the consciousness of the divine love affair that is creation: "I was a hidden treasure and I longed to be loved, so I created the world."

The work of the Sufis and other lovers of God has always been to keep the axis of love pure and protected, so that the world spins on it without distortion, so that His love flows into creation. Through our prayers, our practices, and the openness of our heart, we are present at the axis of love. Our love for God, the love between lover and Beloved, sings along it. In this way we live it in this world.

The lover looks after the axis of love in the world through the simplicity of her devotions, through keeping her heart pure and the attention of the heart turned towards God while she lives her everyday life. How we live the love affair that is creation is unique to each of us. No two ways of love are the same. But every lover lives the same axis of love. It is alive in our hearts, present in each and every breath. And when we remember Him, it sings within us, nourishing life in the most hidden and wonderful ways.

Everything in life is a lover waiting for the Beloved. Just as love draws human lovers together, it draws everything back to union. If there were no love holding creation together, everything would fall apart. Every molecule is part of a play of love and longing that hides and reveals His face. We fulfill our part in this love affair in the simplest of ways—through relating to others with love, through cooking or cleaning with love, through living our daily life with remembrance and awareness, which for the Sufi is the awareness of the heart.

Through this awareness we recognize our Beloved in His world; we see His face in the beauty and the chaos: in a summer sunrise as well as in the rush-hour traffic. Love is within us and within everything we meet: it is in the noise of the alarm clock and the taste of the toast. When we remember Him with our heart, when we repeat His name with devotion, we are the note of love in the world. Our hearts form part of the spinning axis of His love for His world. Our work is to live this axis of love, and to keep it pure just as we keep our heart pure and polished.

There are many distractions that take us away from this work of love. Our psyche offers us endless problems; the world holds so many attractions. And in our culture we think of love as something special, a privilege that some are born into through the gift of a loving parent. We hunt for love in relationships, seek it in friendship or love affairs. We try to give it to our children. We package our idea of love in hopes and disappointments, fears, anxieties, and self-judgments. We enclose it in our psychological problems.

We can follow the discord within us, our lack of self-worth, our jealousies and anger. We can project love outside ourselves and run after the ego's fantasies and desires. Or we can acknowledge the ordinariness of love; we can recognize that love is the primal substance of creation. We can find the thread of love within ourself and within life, and begin to see the many ways His love reveals itself. In the words of Fakhruddîn 'Irâqî,

> His loveliness owns
>   a hundred thousand faces;
> gaze upon a different fair one
>   in every atom;
> for He needs must show
>   to every separate mote
> a different aspect
>   of His Beauty.[2]

Once we look under the surface we can find love everywhere. Part of spiritual practice is to recognize this, to see the thread of love that is woven into everything. Then we consciously participate in the love affair that is life. This is part of the mystery of seeing His face "wheresoever you turn."

When we awaken to the presence of love and begin to relate to all life as a way to love God, then something opens within the human being and we can participate in this mystery of love in the most ordinary everyday things. Opening a car door, picking up a bag of groceries with love and remembrance, we are directly interacting with this love affair of the creation. We are breathing with the breath of God, loving with the love of God in everything we do. In this way we carry the knowing of His love for the world, and help life come alive with the note of love.

His love is not always sweet; often it is bitter, sometimes even mundane. It is simple and so easily overlooked. It is a way to relate to life, a way to recognize what is real, a way to remember Him. And once we glimpse this love, it needs our constant attention; it needs the work of a heart attuned to love. The path prepares us for this work. It attunes our heart to the frequency of His love. The practices of the path polish the heart so that we can awaken within His love. Then we need to live it fully, to "give it blood." This is the remembrance of the heart lived in every breath, in every act. This is our mystical contribution to life.

A NEW NOTE OF DIVINE LOVE

The love at the axis of the world has a vibration or musical note that is central to the mystery of revelation—the way the world reflects its Creator. The world is a place of divine revelation, and this note attunes the creation with the Creator so that He can reveal Himself or veil Himself.

This revelation is not static, but a continually evolving dance of lover and Beloved: "He never reveals Himself in the same form twice." His revelation changes every moment, in each new bud on every tree, in every bird flying across the sky. There are also patterns of revelation; the ways that He reveals Himself change with each new age. This is why every age has its own particular signs of God, and why between the ages there is a period of confusion and transition as the old signs no longer hold meaning and the new signs are not yet recognized.[3]

We are currently in such a time of transition. A new note is waiting now to be infused into creation, to be brought into the axis of love and from there into the whole tapestry of life, the interconnected web of creation. The new note will help align creation with the patterns of revelation that belong to the coming age, and will carry a new vibration that will affect life in a slightly new way.

We have forgotten that spiritual consciousness, like all life, evolves. The note of love in the previous era helped point us to a monotheistic divinity beyond our physical world. A transcendent God was the gift of the patriarchal era, which was marked by a perception of duality: earth and heaven, matter and spirit. Spiritual practices and teachings worked within the context of this understanding, guiding us further and further away from the material world and instinctual life, while knowledge about the physical world was left to the discoveries of science.

Part of the new pattern of revelation is a celebration of His oneness and the sanctity of divine presence.

The note of love of the coming era has the potential of awakening humanity to the divine oneness within all life. The different levels and dimensions of reality will reflect His oneness in a new way. For example, instead of understanding levels of reality as hierarchical, a ladder of spiritual ascent, we might be able to experience all levels as integral parts of a multidimensional whole—nothing is higher or lower in oneness. Since love is everywhere, this new vibration will be able to go to places that have long been forgotten, releasing the light in the depths of matter, for example.

The new note of love is so new that we can hardly imagine what it will reveal. But it is like a key to a new perception. It can awaken centers of power and ways of spiritual perception both within the earth and within humanity that will contribute to a whole new pattern of His revelation, a new relationship between Creator and creation, a new way of living His love.

Part of the work of His lovers at this time is to help to bring it into life. While the heart of the mystic looks towards God, the lover is also present in life: we are a part of the world of creation as well as being awakened to the world of divine command. The mystic is part of the axis of love in the outer and inner worlds, the world of the senses and the world of light. The note of love that is present within our heart is also present in the cells of our body, and is thus brought into the world of creation.

Our physical self, our body and instinctual nature, is part of the whole web of life. It belongs to an interdependent living organism that is our planet. We are all connected in both the inner and outer worlds, part of an interrelated oneness. Through the heart of the mystic the new note of love is brought from the uncreated worlds into the worlds of creation where it is immediately part of life's oneness. The note that sings in the lover sings in all of life. Nothing is excluded.

Before the lover can bring this note into life, she has to be fully aligned with this new pattern. The hearts and also the consciousness of His lovers have to be subtly changed. This work is taking place now. And this realigning happens not just individually but also on a group level: groups of lovers as well as other types of spiritual seekers are being realigned, their inner and outer orientation changed. This is happening because it is through groups of individuals that the spiritual energy needed for the new unfolding can be most easily transmitted. Spiritual groups are spiritual centers of the coming age.[4]

Realigning groups and individuals takes time. We all have our patterns of resistance, our identification with old ways. While the hearts of His lovers may be open, often our patterns of consciousness are more crystallized. Groups also have their patterns and spiritual identities that can become fixed.

The new note of love needs our conscious participation: we need to know that we are a dynamic part of an unfolding oneness that is also a new face of revelation. The new note of love needs also to be a knowing that we are one.

AWAKENING FROM A DREAM

This new note of love comes from the inner, uncreated worlds, the "dark silence" that is near to the Source. From this emptiness galaxies are born, as is the love that sustains them. Lovers and mystics who are inwardly immersed in the uncreated emptiness can have direct access to love that is not constricted by form. Their hearts are a space for this love to come into the world.

So much in the inner worlds is changing. For example, the archetypal structures of life are changing—the pure energy of creation is beginning to flow into new patterns, like water flowing along newly formed riverbeds. And in the plane of oneness, which is the dimension of the Self, human consciousness is becoming more awake to the dynamics of how oneness works.

Changes are also taking place in the uncreated worlds, which contain the invisible forces behind creation. The dazzling darkness, the nothingness beyond the mind, is full of energy that has not yet manifested even into light. Many of the changes that we sense in our outer life, for example newly developing patterns of relationship that function non-hierarchically, have their origins in deep changes taking place in this emptiness.

Just as love is born in the emptiness, so too are the new vibrations of love. A spiritual master who is immersed in these inner dimensions can attune the hearts of his disciples to these vibrations. Then the love that flows from master to disciple will have a slightly different vibration, which will affect the whole being of the disciple. Through the heart and physical body of the disciple this new vibration of love comes into being.

The axis of love is present in everything, just as the name of God is written on every cell of creation. But because this axis is most accessible in the hearts of His lovers—those who have given their lives to loving Him—it is through our hearts that we can bring this new note of love from love's source in the uncreated into life. From the innermost center of our heart, the secret of secrets to which only the Beloved and His servants have access, the note of love comes into the world of creation, into our instinctual nature and physical body.

This note includes everything: there is no differentiation into light or dark, low or high. Everything is a celebration of His love. It is the ability of the lover to bring together the innermost and the outer worlds, all bonded together in love and service, that allows the note of love to be transmitted without discord. The more completely the lover is surrendered in service, the more effortless is this work. When the whole being of the lover completely bows down before the Lord, the note of love resonates effortlessly at its highest frequency.

It is important to include the physical, because the new note of love needs to be heard in the physical body of the world, in the places where our greed and ignorance have polluted and desecrated the earth. This work with the physical belongs particularly to women, because it is through a woman's physical body and being that love flows most easily into the physical world. This is an aspect of the sacred mystery of motherhood, a woman's capacity to give birth. Unlike a man's, a woman's physical body contains the sacred substance of creation. Every woman carries in her cells a light, absent in men's bodies, that allows the light of a soul to take on form through her body, divine love to manifest physically in a new human being. This sacred substance and light that women uniquely carry will also allow the new vibration of love to reach into the physical body of the world.

Love is a language that most of us have forgotten.[5] We think of love as a warm fuzzy feeling, a sense of caring, or a passionate embrace. But love is the most direct connection between the Creator and His creation. Love is how the Creator speaks to His world, and it conveys both knowledge and nourishment. There are so many subtleties to love's language, which speaks to both our souls and our bodies. And part of its wonder is that it can flow through our hearts and into the world without diluting its ability to convey His meaning.

The new note of love is partly like an encoded message that will speak to creation, awakening it from the past centuries' bad dream of pollution and desecration. It will talk to the world about the patterns of oneness that exist within it, and the way the energy of life can flow along these patterns, cleansing and purifying the world. Life has been waiting to hear this secret message from the Creator to His creation. Until it is heard, life cannot awaken. We have forgotten that His love can speak to the world, just as we have long forgotten the sacred and magical connections to the world that exist within women. We have been living our rational dream of separation and isolation until it has become a soul-destroying nightmare.

Just as His love awakens each of us, so it can awaken the world. His love turns the heart and gives us a knowing of what is real. In the light of His love we discover our purpose and learn to live what is sacred within us. Without the touch of His love we remain asleep, knowing only the dream world of the ego. In that dream we follow the cycles of suffering and desire, but when we awake we realize that another world is present around us, a world in which we are given what we need and are nourished by the primal joy of life. When the world awakes, its complex problems will dissolve like a bad dream, as we all realize that there is a way to relate through life's natural connections, through the oneness that is fundamental to all of us.

LIVING LOVE'S NEW NOTE

What does it mean to be awake and receptive to this new note of love? The challenges will be different for each of us. But it will be helpful to remember that this note of divine love is *new*. It does not belong to the spiritual lexicons of the past. It brings together the worlds in a new way. It is a joy waiting to be lived, a new bud on the tree of life. It will touch us in ways that we have not been touched; it will awaken us within a world alive with His presence.

Every part of life speaks to every other part in the language of love, and we can learn this language. We can learn once again how to talk to life and listen to life's response. We can see the patterns of love as they are present in life: the signs that the Beloved has placed in His creation. We can learn to work with the magic and power of love within life—in the oneness that includes everything in the inner and outer worlds, not just in the secret inner spaces of the heart, in meditation or prayer.

To participate in these changes, we must leave behind any pattern of spiritual isolation that might separate us from life or from each other, or any image of hierarchical spiritual ascent. Our Beloved is not a solitary inner figure but a dynamic oneness that embraces the seen and unseen worlds. Living the wholeness of His love means stepping outside any pattern of conditioning into an ever-expanding universe of the created and the uncreated. To live His oneness, rather than focusing solely on our own individual inner journey we have to consciously recognize that we are part of an interdependent whole. Patterns that restrict our unconditional openness to His presence will limit our ability to transmit His love.

All we need to do is acknowledge that we are a part of life and a part of God. Our higher and lower natures contain the worlds. Every cell of our body, every touch of our hands, has the axis of love at its core and the patterns of creation in the way it moves. And the note of love communicates what is real to the whole; it helps to reveal His face in the world.

Living the note of love will take us to the edge of ourselves, into the density of life and the light of the heart. We will see how those things are part of each other, how the light needs the darkness and how we are that darkness. And we will sense that something new is coming into being, within us and within the world.

This is not a spiritual exercise but something that we have been waiting for. To be alive at the center of life in this moment of time is a blessing as we help the world throw off the dust of a thousand years. Sufis are sweepers, sweeping up the dust of the world, and there is much work to be done!

We are sweeping away the dust of forgetfulness and the debris of the last patriarchal era. We are bringing the new note of love from the depths of our hearts into the thoroughfares of the world. And we are learning to look at life through the eye of the heart, a consciousness attuned to the new note of love that enables us to see His revelation. In the midst of life He is making Himself known in a new way. Our Beloved is unveiling Himself once again and He needs to be seen, His hidden treasure needs to be known. The mystic is the eyes and ears of God and can read the book of life for Him. But we need to be awake, to be fully alive, in order to read the book of life as it is being written anew.

The book of life is our own life. The new note of love is being born in our own life, allowing us to see and experience our Beloved in a new way. A central core of this experience is the revelation of His oneness in the midst of His world. Nothing is separate, nothing is excluded. Every breath is His breath. We can see life through the eyes of the ego, which tells its story of unfulfilled desires, isolation, and patterns of protection, or we can recognize that another story is being told in which our individual self is part of the whole of creation. This interconnected, living wonder includes the addict and his needle and the child and her new toy: we are the spider and its bite and the hummingbird and its taste of nectar. We are life in all its manifold expressions of the One. We are here to experience the fullness of life and know that it is God.

Every day, every moment, we have to say "Yes" to our Beloved and His life. In this primal "Yes" we celebrate His presence in our life and in the world. We are not here to change the world, but to experience it through His eyes of revelation. Then we will see that it has already changed, and what most people imagine as life is just the fading images of the previous era. Looking through the patterns of conditioning, we see a dying world destroying itself with greed and pollution. Through the eyes of revelation, we will see a new world forming amidst these shadows.

Through our "Yes" we claim our right to see with the light of the new, to experience what is being born. And then, in a moment both so simple and so extraordinary, we will realize that we are what is being born. In the miracle of His oneness the center of life is within us; the mystery of life happens in every moment for each of us. We are the center of the circle. We are our Beloved revealing Himself anew.

Epilogue

We make the soul's journey for His sake, because He has called us, because He has awakened in our heart the memory of when we were together with Him. We are polishing our heart for the sake of His love, freeing ourself from illusions and the grip of the ego until we can see the secrets of His oneness. Then we will know why we are here. Our Beloved has called us out of forgetfulness into remembrance and He needs us to bring His light into the world.

There is only one presence, only one Beloved. He whom we love is always with us, because we are a part of Him. We are the vast ocean and the blade of grass. We are the drunkard staggering home at night and the child waiting for the school bus. And we are our own ordinary self, feeling better after a cup of coffee in the morning. And we are also the world waiting before dawn, tired of the darkness, needing the light of the souls of His lovers to awaken.

In the light of His oneness, life is as it has always been. Fruit grows on the fruit tree and is sold in the marketplace. The cycle of life continues. But something is different. Something has come into being that was not here before—something is visible that was hidden. What has changed, what is new? Something His lovers know within their hearts is being given to the world. Part of His secret self is being made visible. How this will change our world hangs in the balance.

We are here at a moment in time and we *are* this moment, each alive in our own way. Watch carefully and you can see what is being given, what is being passed from heart to heart, from soul to soul. Something new is being made known, and we are a part of it. We are a secret being born, a new way of praise and prayer that includes all of creation, that is a celebration of divine oneness. And before the tide turns and this moment is gone, we need to plant the seed of this prayer into the depths of the earth, into the places of power, into the currents of love that flow through the earth. Then the world can awaken.

NOTES

TITLE PAGES

1. "The Mother Womb Creates the Human," Babylonian-Assyrian, *Desert Wisdom*, Neil Douglas-Klotz, p. 24.

CHAPTER 1: THE FIRST STEP

1. See the work of Peter Kingsley, www.peterkingsley.org.
2. The Bible, *Gospel of Mark* 2:22.

CHAPTER 2: SPIRITUAL MATURITY

1. "Poems of the Sufi Way," *'Umar Ibn al-Fârid: Sufi Verse, Saintly Life*, p. 269.
2. *Four Quartets*, "Little Gidding," ll. 253-254.
3. Junayd was the essence of patience. When Shiblî first encountered Junayd, he demanded,
   > "You are recommended as an expert on pearls....Either give me one or sell one to me."
   >
   > "If I sell you one, you will not have the price of it, and if I give you one, having come so easily by it, you will not realize its value," Junaid replied. "Do like me; plunge headfirst into this Sea, and if you wait patiently you will obtain your pearl."
   >
   > Shiblî had to wait many years and perform numerous tasks before Junaid accepted him as a disciple. (Mohammad Shafii, *Freedom from the Self*, pp. 218-219.)
4. *Early Islamic Mysticism*, p. 206.
5. There is a darkness and negative energy around such places that can attack spiritual consciousness, just as indiscriminate sex can disturb the balance of one's psychic and spiritual centers.

CHAPTER 3: COLLIDING FORCES

1. "Her Triumph," *Collected Poems of W. B. Yeats*, p. 310.
2. "The Second Coming," *Collected Poems of W. B. Yeats*, p. 210.
3. Later, the empire founded by Ghengis Khan created an environment that encouraged trade, the exchange of ideas, and religious tolerance.
4. See Peter Kingsley, *Reality*, for a fuller exploration of *metis* in the teaching of the ancient Greeks.
5. The popularity of the *Harry Potter* series points to our longing for a world not restricted by the blindness of the "muggles."

CHAPTER 4: THE RELATIONSHIP BETWEEN THE WORLDS

1. In Indian yoga the world of creation belongs to the first three centers of consciousness, or *chakras* (the root-, the sexual-, and the solar-plexus *chakra*), while the four higher centers (the heart-, the throat-, the brow-, and the crown *chakra*) belong to spiritual consciousness. Most people function with the three lower *chakras*, while the four higher centers are awakened through spiritual practice.
2. In yoga these energy drives are associated respectively with the three lower *chakras*.
3. *First Epistle of Paul to the Corinthians* 13:12.
4. See pp. 96 & 97.
5. Najm al-Dîn Razî, *The Path of God's Bondsmen*, trans. Hamid Algar, p. 147.
6. *Psalm* 36:9.
7. Not all darkness is to be transformed into light. Creation needs the density of darkness, its force of contraction. We know how our own darkness contracts us, how our fears constrict us, how selfishness draws us into ourself and hardens us. Our darkness holds our light here in this world. Through our darkness we belong to the forces of the earth, the limitations of time, matter, and form. This is the archetype of Saturn or Kronos, the cruel god who devoured his children. Contraction, limitation, crystallization, the survival instinct, self-preservation, the constriction of spirit into matter are all aspects of this primal energy of the earth which we need to counter the natural expansiveness of spirit.
8. *Epistle of Paul to the Galatians* 5:17.
9. *Kundalini* energy is experienced by most people in the form of sexual energy, which is the creative power of God. The Sufi master Bhai Sahib explains that an impotent man or woman cannot realize the Truth: "A man who is impotent can never be a Saint or a Yogi. Women too can

be impotent. The Creative Energy of God which manifests itself in its lowest aspect as procreative instinct is the most powerful thing in human beings, men and women alike" (Irina Tweedie, *Daughter of Fire*, p. 149).

10. "If there were no *Prakriti* [matter], there would be no Light. The more sex-power the human being has, the easier he will reach God or Truth. Impotent people cannot have *Brahma Vidya*, men or women. Great sex power is a great help in spiritual life. The outcome, the emanation of *Brahma Vidya* is coming down into manifestation as *Virya Shakti*, the Creative Energy of God" (*Daughter of Fire*, p. 497).

11. Vaughan-Lee, *The Circle of Love*, ch. 3 and 4, pp. 37-82, explore in detail the psychological dynamics of claiming the power we need for spiritual life.

12. *Matthew* 10:16.

13. According to Paracelsus, *lumen naturae* is associated with the knowledge of natural magic, the magic of the physical world. "Magic," he says, "is the preceptor and teacher of the physician, who derives his knowledge from the *lumen naturae*." C. G. Jung, *Collected Works*, vol. 8, ¶ 148.

14. *The Path of God's Bondsmen*, p. 363.

CHAPTER 5: ANIMA MUNDI: AWAKENING THE SOUL OF THE WORLD

1. Stephan Hoeller, *Gnosis: A Journal of Western Inner Traditions* (vol. 8, Summer 1988).

2. Timaeus 30D3-31A1, *Plato's Timaeus*, trans. F. M. Cornford.

3. There is a tradition that medieval stained-glass makers were taught by alchemists how to use glass to transform light.

4. David Fideler, *The Soul of the Cosmos*, p. 138. Richard Tarnas, *The Passion of the Western Mind*, p. 213.

5. Giordano Bruno, *Cause, Principle, and Unity*, trans. Jack Lindsay, p. 81.

6. Alchemical text quoted by C. G. Jung, *Collected Works*, vol. 8, p. 388.

7. C. G. Jung, *Collected Works*, vol. 14, p. 372.

8. See John Eberly, *Al-Kima: The Mystical Islamic Essence of the Sacred Art of Alchemy*.

9. *The Hermetic Museum*, 1:13, quoted by Edward Edinger in *The Anatomy of the Psyche*, p. 11. See also Vaughan-Lee, *Catching the Thread*, p. 66ff.

10. Quoted by Edinger, *Anatomy of the Psyche*, p. 231. Hermes Trismegistos is the "patron" of the alchemical art. According to legend, the original Emerald Tablet was found in the tomb of Hermes Trismegistos by

Alexander the Great. "It is the cryptic epitome of the alchemical *opus*, a recipe for the second creation of the world, the *unus mundus*."

11. *Poems and Prose of Gerard Manley Hopkins*, "God's Grandeur."

12. Ghalib, trans. Jane Hirshfield, *The Enlightened Heart*, ed. Stephen Mitchell, p. 105.

13. C. G. Jung, *Collected Works*, vol. 11, p. 759.

14. David Fideler, *The Soul of the Cosmos*, p. 100.

15. http://en.wikipedia.org/wiki/The_Garden_of_Cyrus.

16. Paul Oskar Kristeller, *The Philosophy of Marsilio Ficino*, p. 120.

17. Hermes Trismegistos, *The Emerald Tablet*, 4 & 5.

18. "Therefore you should carefully test and examine the life, character, and mental aptitude of any person who would be initiated in this Art." *The Hermetic Museum*, 2:12. Quoted by Edward Edinger, *Anatomy of the Psyche*, p. 7.

19. E. E. Cummings, *Selected Poems 1923-1958*, "i thank You God for most this amazing."

CHAPTER 6: THE LIGHT OF THE HEART

1. *Three Early Sufi Texts*, p. 52.

2. C. G. Jung, *Collected Works*, vol. 14, *Mysterium Coniunctionis*, ¶ 554.

3. William Chittick, *The Sufi Path of Knowledge*, p. 17.

4. *Katha Upanishad*, Book II, 1, *Ten Principle Upanishads*, trans. Shree Purohit Swami and W. B. Yeats, p. 34.

5. *Three Early Sufi Texts*, p. 35.

6. Naqshbandis differentiated among five *latâ'if* belonging to the world of God's command ('*âlâm-e amr*)—heart (*qalb*), spirit (*rûh*), secret (*sirr*), hidden (*khafî*), and most hidden (*akhfâ*)—and five *latâ'if* belonging to the world of creation (*âlâm-e kalq*)—self (*nafs*), air (*hâd*), fire (*nâr*), water (*mâ*), and earth (*khâk*). Each *latîfah* is associated with a color and a specific location in the body.

7. Arthur F. Buehler, *Sufi Heirs of the Prophet*, p. 110.

8. Quoted by Ibn 'Arabî. See William Chittick, *The Sufi Path of Knowledge*, p. 103.

9. Quoted in Irina Tweedie, *Daughter of Fire*, p. 180.

10. The archetypal or symbolic world is traditionally seen as an intermediary plane between the physical world of the senses and the world of the soul, the plane of pure being. It is most easily accessed through the faculty of "active" or "creative" imagination. See Vaughan-Lee, *Working with Oneness*, ch. 8: "Imagination," pp. 111–124.

11. See Vaughan-Lee, *Spiritual Power*.

CHAPTER 7: THE AXIS OF LOVE

1. Quoted by Claude Addas, "The Experience and Doctrine of Love in Ibn 'Arabî," *Sufi*, Issue 63, Autumn 2004, p. 24.
2. Fakhruddîn 'Irâqî, *Divine Flashes*, p. 81.
3. See Vaughan-Lee, *The Signs of God*, in particular the final chapter, "Recognizing the Signs of God."
4. See Vaughan-Lee, *In the Company of Friends*.
5. See Vaughan-Lee, *Spiritual Power*, ch. 7: "The Language of Love," pp. 122-141.

BIBLIOGRAPHY

Addas, Claude. "The Experience and Doctrine of Love in Ibn 'Arabî," *Sufi*, Issue 63, Autumn 2004.

The Bible, Authorized Version. London: 1611.

Buehler, Arthur F. *Sufi Heirs of the Prophet*. Columbia, SC: University of South Carolina, 1998.

Bruno, Giordano. *Cause, Principle, and Unity: Five Dialogues*. Trans. Jack Lindsay. New York: International Publishers, 1964.

Chittick, William. *The Sufi Path of Love*. Albany, NY: State University of New York Press, 1983.

—. *The Sufi Path of Knowledge*. Albany, NY: State University of New York Press, 1989.

Cummings, E. E. *Selected Poems 1923-1958*. London: Faber and Faber, 1960.

Douglas-Klotz, Neil. *Desert Wisdom*. New York: Harper Collins, 1995.

Eberly, John. *Al-Kima*. Hillsdale, NY: Sophia Perennis, 2004.

Edinger, Edward. *Anatomy of the Psyche*. La Salle, IL: Open Court Publishing, 1985.

Eliot, T.S. *Collected Poems*. London: Faber and Faber, 1963.

Fideler, David. *The Soul of the Cosmos*. Unpublished work.

Hoeller, Stephan. *Gnosis: A Journal of Western Inner Traditions*, vol. 8, Summer 1988.

Hopkins, Gerard Manley. *The Poems and Prose of Gerard Manley Hopkins*. Harmondsworth: Penguin Books, 1953.

Ibn al-Fârid, 'Umar.'*Umar Ibn al-Fârid: Sufi Verse, Saintly Life*. Trans. Th. Emil Homerin. New York: Paulist Press, 2001.

'Irâqî, Fakhruddîn. *Divine Flashes*. Trans. Peter Lamborn Wilson. New York: Paulist Press, 1982.

Jung, C. G. *Collected Works*. London: Routledge & Kegan Paul.

Kingsley, Peter. *Reality*. Inverness, CA: The Golden Sufi Center, 2004.

Kristeller, Paul Oskar. *Philosophy of Marsilio Ficino*. New York: Columbia University Press,1984.

Mitchell, Stephen, ed. *The Enlightened Heart*. New York: Harper & Row, 1989.

Plato. *Plato's Timaeus*. Trans. F. M. Cornford. Indianapolis, IN: Bobbs-Merrill, 1959.

Razî, Najm al-Dîn. *The Path of God's Bondsmen*. Trans. Hamid Algar. North Haledon, NJ: Islamic Publications International, 1980.

Sells, Michael, ed. *Early Islamic Mysticism*. New York: Paulist Press, 1996.

Shafii, Mohammad. *Freedom from the Self*. New York: Human Science Press, 1985.

Tirmidhî, Al-Hakîm Al-. *Three Early Sufi Texts*. Trans. Nicholas Heer. Louisville, KY: Fons Vitae, 2003.

Tweedie, Irina. *Daughter of Fire: A Diary of a Spiritual Training with a Sufi Master*. Nevada City, CA: Blue Dolphin Publishing, 1986.

Vaughan-Lee, Llewellyn. *Spiritual Power: How It Works*. Inverness, CA: The Golden Sufi Center, 2005.

—. *Working with Oneness*. Inverness, CA: The Golden Sufi Center, 2002.

—. *The Signs of God*. Inverness, CA: Golden Sufi Center, 2001.

—. *The Circle of Love*. Inverness, CA: Golden Sufi Center, 1999.

—. *In the Company of Friends*. Inverness, CA: Golden Sufi Center, 1994.

Yeats, W. B. *Collected Poems of W. B. Yeats*. London: Macmillan, 1933.

—. Trans. (with Shree Purohit Swami). *The Ten Principal Upanishads*. London: Faber and Faber, 1937.

INDEX

Y

Yeats, W. B. (d. 1939) 36, 38,
     130, 132

Z

Zen 23

ACKNOWLEDGMENTS

For permission to use copyrighted material, the author gratefully wishes to acknowledge: Liveright Publishing Corporation, for permission to quote lines from "i thank You God for most this amazing". Copyright 1950, © 1978, 1991 by the Trustees for the E. E. Cummings Trust. Copyright © 1979 by George James Firmage, from *Complete Poems: 1904-1962* by E. E. Cummings, edited by George J. Firmage; Paulist Press (www.paulistpress.com) for excerpts from *Divine Flashes* by Fakhruddîn 'Irâqî © 1982 The Missionary Society of St. Paul the Apostle in the State of New York, *Early Islamic Mysticism*, edited by Michael Sells © 1996 Michael Sells, and *'Umar Ibn al-Fârid: Sufi Verse, Saintly Life*, translated by Th. Emil Homerin © 2001 Th. Emil Homerin; Islamic Publications International for excerpts from *The Path of God's Bondsmen* by Najm al-Dîn Razî, translated by Hamid Algar © 1980 Center for Iranian Studies, Columbia University; Neil Douglas-Klotz, for permission to quote selection from "The Mother Womb Creates the Human" from *Desert Wisdom: Native Middle Eastern Writing from the Goddess through the Sufis* copyright © 1995 Neil Douglas-Klotz, all rights reserved, Abwoon Study Circle: www.abwoon.com

ABOUT *the* AUTHOR

LLEWELLYN VAUGHAN-LEE, Ph.D., is a Sufi Teacher in the Naqshbandiyya-Mujaddidiyya Sufi Order. Born in London in 1953, he has followed the Naqshbandi Sufi path since he was 19. In 1991 he moved to Northern California and became the successor of Irina Tweedie, author of *Chasm of Fire* and *Daughter of Fire*. In recent years the focus of his writing and teaching has been on spiritual responsibility in our present time of transition, and the emerging global consciousness of oneness (see www.workingwithoneness.org). He has also specialized in the area of dreamwork, integrating the ancient Sufi approach to dreams with the insights of modern psychology. Author of several books, Llewellyn lectures throughout the United States and Europe.

ABOUT *the* PUBLISHER

THE GOLDEN SUFI CENTER is a California Religious Non-Profit Corporation dedicated to making the teachings of the Naqshbandi Sufi path available to all seekers. For further information about the activities and publications, please contact:

THE GOLDEN SUFI CENTER
P.O. Box 428
Inverness, CA 94937-0428
tel: 415-663-8773 · *fax:* 415-663-9128
info@goldensufi.org · www.goldensufi.org

ADDITIONAL PUBLICATIONS
from THE GOLDEN SUFI CENTER

by IRINA TWEEDIE
DAUGHTER OF FIRE:
A Diary of a Spiritual Training with a Sufi Master

⁓

by LLEWELLYN VAUGHAN-LEE
SPIRITUAL POWER:
How It Works

MOSHKEL GOSHA:
A Story of Transformation

WORKING WITH ONENESS

THE SIGNS OF GOD

LOVE IS A FIRE:
The Sufi's Mystical Journey Home

THE CIRCLE OF LOVE

CATCHING THE THREAD:
Sufism, Dreamwork, and Jungian Psychology

THE FACE BEFORE I WAS BORN:
A Spiritual Autobiography

THE PARADOXES OF LOVE

SUFISM, THE TRANSFORMATION OF THE HEART

IN THE COMPANY OF FRIENDS:
Dreamwork within a Sufi Group

THE BOND WITH THE BELOVED:
The Mystical Relationship of the Lover and the Beloved

⁓

edited by LLEWELLYN VAUGHAN-LEE
with biographical information by SARA SVIRI
TRAVELLING THE PATH OF LOVE:
Sayings of Sufi Masters

⁓

by PETER KINGSLEY
REALITY

IN THE DARK PLACES OF WISDOM

⁓

by SARA SVIRI
THE TASTE OF HIDDEN THINGS:
Images of the Sufi Path

⁓

by HILARY HART
THE UNKNOWN SHE:
Eight Faces of an Emerging Consciousness

⁓

ABOUT WORKING *with* ONENESS

www.workingwithoneness.org

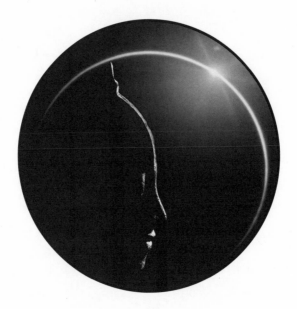

This site is dedicated to connecting with spiritual groups of all types who are working towards the emerging consciousness of oneness. Consciousness of oneness is an awareness of the unity and interconnectedness of all of life. This is central to our human and planetary survival and evolution.

At the present time there is a greater need for those of us drawn to this work of oneness to connect with each other. We hope this website will be a valuable resource for you in facilitating this connection.

Please visit our website, www.workingwithoneness.org for information on upcoming events and publications, or contact us at info@workingwithoneness.org.